HOW TO BUILD
A MODEL RAILWAY

HOW TO BUILD
A MODEL RAILWAY

An Introduction to the Hobby

David Ashwood

&

The Market Deeping Model Railway Club, CIO

PEN & SWORD
TRANSPORT

AN IMPRINT OF PEN & SWORD BOOKS LTD.
YORKSHIRE - PHILADELPHIA

First published in Great Britain in 2022 by
Pen and Sword Transport
An imprint of
Pen & Sword Books Ltd.
Yorkshire - Philadelphia

ISBN 978 1 39909 484 9

Typeset in 11.5/14 Palatino
by SJmagic DESIGN SERVICES, India.

Printed and bound in India by Replika Press Pvt. Ltd.

Pen & Sword Books Ltd incorporates the imprints of Pen & Sword Books Archaeology, Atlas, Aviation, Battleground, Discovery, Family History, History, Maritime, Military, Naval, Politics, Railways, Select, Transport, True Crime, Fiction, Frontline Books, Leo Cooper, Praetorian Press, Seaforth Publishing, Wharncliffe and White Owl.

For a complete list of Pen & Sword titles please contact

PEN & SWORD BOOKS LIMITED
47 Church Street, Barnsley, South Yorkshire, S70 2AS, England
E-mail: enquiries@pen-and-sword.co.uk
Website: www.pen-and-sword.co.uk

or

PEN AND SWORD BOOKS
1950 Lawrence Rd, Havertown, PA 19083, USA
E-mail: Uspen-and-sword@casematepublishers.com
Website: www.penandswordbooks.com

Contents

1
Introduction

Some modellers are able to start from scratch, where everything is shiny and new. Real life also has the same opportunity. This is the interior of Norwich Thorpe diesel maintenance depot taken prior to its formal opening on 28 June 1956. Some Derby Lightweight units are unmarshalled at this point and Hunslet 0-6-0 shunter 11141 propels another on the centre road ready for the press release next day. Our aim in this book is to show how to build a model railway, but we have also taken the opportunity to include some previously unpublished prototype images to fire your imagination. (*Meredith 369-9 Online Transport Archive*)

This Happy Breed of Men, This Little World

The Market Deeping Model Railway Club (MDMRC) was formed in 1976, the year *Concorde* took to the skies. The Club, in common with all of its ilk, is a thriving social ecosystem of likeminded railway modellers, with a desire to learn, share, specialise and display the end results to the public at exhibitions. The pictures on the following pages are taken from a combination of Club and home layouts belonging to members and represent the broad spectrum of this hobby, from the smallest display, through child-friendly layouts to larger, longer-term builds.

Like so many that exist in the United Kingdom, this Club has an interesting mix of contributing careers, a can-do attitude and a structure of 'officers' that can cope with planning and budgeting through to handling the most unexpected of circumstances. Indeed, the Club would have been termed as 'proficient but unexceptional' among its peers, until disaster struck on the night of 17 May 2019.

The Annual Model Railway Show was set up at a school in the idyllic town of Stamford, Lincolnshire, on a Friday night, ready for an early start the next morning. All hands were on deck, a hive of activity after the school closed for the day. Layouts were set up and tested, 'position one' rolling stock put in place. Traders arrived and their wares were set out ready to sell on their displays.

During the night the school sports hall was invaded, and an extensive spree of vandalism occurred.

At 6:30 am the school caretaker with the author and his wife, who were simply expecting to make the morning's breakfast rolls, instead opened up to discover most of the contents had been comprehensively reduced to matchwood. Our own layouts, those of fellow clubs and the traders' stalls were all demolished.

It was the last thing you would expect to see. In some cases, twenty-five years of work were gone; kindly men over seventy were in tears. The Club and all others present experienced shock, anger and disbelief. That Saturday afternoon

The shocking aftermath of the Club main display located in a school sports hall that fateful Saturday morning. You can make out parts of layouts and displays, but it certainly does not look as expected for a public open day. Parallels exist in general for those building home railouts. You are making an investment of time and money. At least a financial value can be got back through having correct insurance. There are named extensions to home policies and specialist coverage for accidental damage and theft which are worth considering. If you price up the replacement value of a collection it can be a surprising total. Outside sheds should be alarmed, layout and working areas should have a powder or gas electrical fire extinguisher provided. (*MDMRC*)

was spent with brooms and dustbins, and we wondered just where we would go to cope with the damage and loss of club earnings. We decided to set up a £500 'Just Giving' request online to offset losses.

During the following week news of the vandalism was flashed around the world, seizing the common imagination. Club members appeared on television and radio. Our one operable locomotive, taken from a raffle prize, was set up on our Club's test track to show some background movement.

Within a day, members of the rail modelling fraternity, wargamers, the general public, people with fond memories of their grandfathers' past, provided kind words, and donations of all kinds poured in. From Miniatur Wonderland of Hamburg and Sir Rod Stewart through to children's pocket money and a lady from Japan apologising for her English. It should be realised that there was not only the financial investment, but the irreplaceable time and devotion of passed and older members, ideas, aspirations, discovery – all had been lost.

As an end result, the Club decided to form into a charity to handle those kind donations

correctly, to curate a historical collection of assets representing the hobby, to promote school model railway clubs for children and assist other local causes, proving good can come from bad.

Why was this book written? It is a part of the healing process. Our share of any profit from the book will go directly back into the Club charity fund.

This publication is aimed at sharing the successes, perils and pitfalls of taking a model railway beyond a box that is occasionally taken from the cupboard to be set up on the dining table or, if floor based, in, shall we say, 'treadable' format. It is about making the jump to a permanent definition of the owner's dreams, big or small.

We will attempt to demystify the construction of a model railway and show that you do not have to be a carpenter, engineer, planner, historian or DIYer. Taking well considered decisions at the right time can save time, money and ease frustration.

Many people have dreams that have been carried forward from childhood with false starts, or the family life cycle has led to

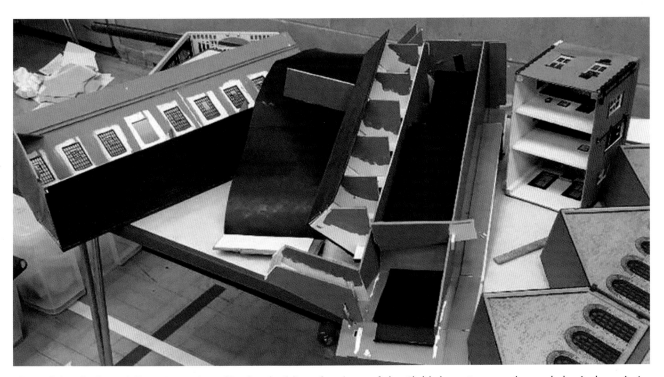

The sad detail of vandalism. Examples of broken buildings from one of the Club's layouts, many beyond physical repair. In the end we tried to recycle as much as possible: parts become donors for later projects and lived in a box in the interim. Saving what you can alleviates feelings of loss and frustration. The same is true for an individual's personal legacy of layout attempts and false starts. Satisfaction can be got from making use of the 'kit-bashing box', stock that does not work or is outdated, spare transfers, bits of wood, odds and ends of materials that live in the shed or loft. (*MDMRC*)

interrupted collections sitting in the attic or the shed. Others have a clean slate to choose from without such baggage where the breadth of choice is perhaps bewildering.

The author is a good example of a blend of both approaches. Teenage attempts at baseboards for OO, which were bulky and could not move from the bedroom, resulted in eventual demolition and boxing of assets. During family life, 1:1 scale trains were played with for many happy years at a museum MPD site in Southall, West London, while smaller trains lived in the loft. As a part time trader, I sold diecast models and kits at shows to keep the dream alive (accompanied by my wife, who by osmosis, now knows a scary amount of railway facts). Then I was a member of the Market Deeping Model Railway Club, with approaching retirement and chose O gauge for the first time for portable and garden layouts. At the time of writing, we have taken advantage of the Covid-19 lockdown to extend a rather large OO Euston Station Club layout which will form the core of another book. The saved models from childhood still exist, on which to practise techniques and build cameos. A robust Hornby Dublo extended diecast set serves to entertain and gently initiate grandchildren into the hobby.

Books such as this cannot exist in pure isolation. They serve as a launch pad for greater things – reading magazines, using the library service, searching the internet, visiting model shows and asking questions. Model shop owners and layout exhibitors get lonely, and they often love to talk. Above all, enjoy yourself in discovering the pleasure of a perfect little world where the trains will always run on time.

Our thanks go to Pen & Sword Books for taking the brave move to involve another facet of the modelling hobby beyond the military and technical. Their extensive coverage is sure to tempt anyone that has looked twice, longingly, at a museum exhibit or a model kit.

Thank you to members of the Market Deeping Club for their kind assistance and willingness to share and advise and to my wife and Club members Peter Davies and Alan Hancock for review and guidance.

2

Decision Making

Would it be better to start small and build your skills? Just post-nationalisation but still badged as LNER at London Stratford works, Class Y11 Simplex 0-4-0 petrol engine shunter 8189 on 13 November 1948. In the background, among others being repainted 'British Railways', is GER N7 0-6-2T 69634, later a stalwart of 30B Hertford East shed. (*Meredith 49-6 Online Transport Archive*)

Making the Correct Decision

You have just returned from a model railway show, fired up with enthusiasm accompanied by a modicum of trepidation and have started making spontaneous investments in rolling stock, perhaps some track or a 'point and shoot'

themed package. Then you stop dead. Where do you go from here? How can you make that jump from a box under the bed to something of a more permanent nature?

You really are not alone. Let us take a brief look back to the embryonic railways of Britain in the 1820s to make some comparisons with your current situation. It is 1826, the Liverpool and Manchester Railway has garnered investment for a 30-mile line between the two major centres as an outlet for manufactured goods. Surveying and land purchase has followed a share issue and commitment formalised via an Act of Parliament.

A builder has been appointed by the Board of Directors, in this case George Stephenson – an adept engineer who can read yet never mastered the art of writing. The 30 miles of track will be constructed by a large manual workforce who will overcome obstacles largely by trial and error. The experiences will be carried over as improvements to time, materials and lives saved as 'railway mania' takes off later in the next decade.

Awaiting construction are sixty-two bridges, 13 miles of substantial cuttings and embankments, four large tunnels, the world's first major viaduct over the Sankey Valley, the Olive Mount Cutting and the 5-mile floating embankment over the Chat Moss peat bog.

Certain stages of decisions, planning and execution are reached to make it successful and viable, and the same is true of your own model requirements. We will share the Club experiences of each stage in this book.

Above left and above right: Olive Mount Cutting near Liverpool. Two miles of sandstone hewn by hand to break through to the city and provide a level trackbed. Picture chicken wire and plaster of Paris or polystyrene cut to make a cutting. (*Wiki Commons*)

Right: Contemporary painting of the Chat Moss embankment. It was constructed by workers who needed planks tied to their boots in the boggy ground, and consisted of a raft of reeds and wood with soil and aggregates on top. As trains pass today there is an 8cm bounce in the track. The same scale behaviour in a model will result in uncoupling and derailment – a firm base is always needed. (*Wiki Commons*)

Your own legacy

The chances are that somewhere in your past you had a train set. It was basic. It went round and round. Family and friends contributed to it and eventually it went into the attic or shed for safe storage and a promise of 'one day'.

This and any new or second-hand goods you purchased along the way become your legacy. It is often difficult to get past the feeling of not wanting to waste money or break an emotional attachment. If the technology or level of detail involved is suitable for your needs, you can easily acquire extra to expand and build on an earlier investment.

However, beware: you may be better off stepping back, keeping your train set as a memento *only* and moving on to something that suits your current circumstances.

You can then use as leverage any improvements in your skills, having honed them on twenty years of Airfix kits or putting in a new kitchen, among the many other things adulthood throws at you to sharpen you up.

The following photographs are a trip down memory lane from our Club archives.

The changes in packaging over the years from the 'Binns Road' Hornby Dublo tabletop railway prior to widespread plastics, through the 'Lines Bros' Triang years (when Freightliner was a glossy XP64 dream with BR and Seawheel) right through to today's bright 'Smoky Joe' type of starter set.

Hornby through the years with the Christmas type of present. A full circuit of a detailed theme with extras such as accessories and buildings to keep you happy until Boxing Day morning. Then you would move a little away from parental controlled prototype, running into the realm of experimental collisions with Lego (or in the author's case dropping soldier figures down the chute from the iron ore wagons).

HO box sets such as these by Fleischmann and Roco, and special rakes of detailed wagons and trains in smaller scales. Are European children a little more caring in their play or the adults profligate? These tend to be expensive and very detailed starter sets.

The reasons for choosing a certain theme are many and various. One Club member has never been to the USA but models that country in HO and N gauges. The reason for this was a rugby team trip to Canada. After a hard-fought day, a bar gave its siren call, only for a huge freight train from south of the border to come in between. How long did it take to get past? Answer: six pints! Another member belonged to a railway preservation group and 'accidentally' purchased LMS brake van M731211 from the electrification team about to scrap stock on the Southall MPD sidings. From that point it was all things Euston for models, despite living and working on Great Western lines.

The evolution of the model railway catalogue, from tinplate 1953 to DCC 2019, books full of dreams.

Method of Control

Today there are two main options to choose from as to how the power gets to your locomotives and accessories.

DC: Direct current

In DC systems, power is fed into the rail lines from a transformer via a controller. The same power source hits any locomotive on the line being powered if it has not been isolated. You will need to provide some power isolation or certain switches and turnouts must be of an isolating type. It means a fair amount of control wiring and switching is required should a complicated setup be desired.

Pros
- At its simplest it is 'plug and play' from a transformer, a controller (sometimes existing together) and two wires.
- It is comparatively cheap.
- It is future-proof as it uses basic technology.
- Robust transformers can give good control.

Cons
- Complex requirements = complex wiring.
- Fault finding can be a challenge.
- Lack of 'real' effect extras.

DCC: digital command control

DCC systems use 'chipset' based digital technology to pass messages through the track to activate locomotive movements, sound and lights.

Each locomotive or accessory requires a chip to be triggered allowing independent control.

Pros
- Flexible operation is comparatively easy.
- A complex wiring loom is not needed.
- Imparts a feeling of command and control.
- Awards more perceived realism.
- You can use an iPad or Android to perform cab control.

Cons
- Expensive technology for each controlled element.
- Technology moves fast and will evolve away from investment over time.
- Incompatibility with some earlier products.
- Complicated assignment setup and use.

Gauge and Scale Considerations

If you have no previous baggage or encumbrances or have chosen to undertake a new project, you need to decide which scale and gauge to work with, to avoid being disappointed or frustrated at the other end. You have certain restrictions of space available, a feel of the complexity or detail desired, the amount you are willing to spend and the availability of materials for your desired prototype.

We need to decrypt some jargon, and it is best to do this by explaining the relative measurements involved and the historical reasons behind the myriad of scales and gauge combinations that exist in the hobby today.

Above left and above right: When dealing with scale you have to remember that all dimensions and volume change by the same ratio. For example, the O (Pocket Money kit) and OO (Hornby) 'Jinty' 3F steam locos, or the BR Class 08 O (Han Sheng Brass) and OO (Lima) diesel electric shunters. It can help greatly to visit a model shop or a model railway exhibition to see the real thing before committing to purchases.

Explaining scales

Scale represents a ratio or size whereas gauge represents the rail gap normally based upon standard gauge (in Britain 4ft 8½in). Over time they have been used interchangeably, bringing confusion.

At the dawn of the model railway hobby, O gauge was the smallest that could be engineered for consistent quality and a low price. The hobby has been complicated by a mixture of imperial and metric measurements between producers in the USA, Europe and historically in the UK. For example, in O gauge 7mm (approx. ¼in) represents 1ft, or a ratio of 1:43, which means that 1in on the model is 43in on the full size item.

There are other larger scales, such as gauge 1, which is ⅜in to 1ft scale (1:32), followed by gauges 2 and 3 until you reach the model engineers' sizes which are still expressed as the actual gauge used, such as 5½ or 7¼in and tend to be outdoor live steam and ride-on options.

As technology improved in Europe and the USA a scale was produced called 'half O', known today as HO, which is 3.5mm to the foot (or 1:87).

Historically, the UK took an alternative route. Because the loading gauge on British railways is smaller than that of Europe, the rolling stock looked undersize in comparison. So to trick the eye, OO scale – which is 4mm to the foot (1:76)

was promoted. HO and OO make use of the same gauge of track: 16.5mm.

Railway modelling did not evolve in a vacuum. Other parts of the modelling hobby adopted different ratio scales, so while wargamers produce some nice 1:72, 1:48 or 1:32 scale scenic models they can be a challenge to adapt to British outline.

Likewise, if you take some HO and OO scenic models and try to mix and match, you can have a frustrating time unless you position them to make a forced perspective with larger in front and smaller behind. Not impossible, but it does take some planning.

Miniaturisation after the Second World War brought TT ('tabletop') gauge from the Triang company. This set a standard at 3mm to the foot. It proved not to be a success commercially, although a 3mm Society still exists today.

The natural halving of scale resulted in N gauge in the 1960s (initially marketed in the UK as 'OOO' by Lone Star). N stands for *neun* (nine in German), which is the gauge in mm (9mm), as defined by the German Arnold company, who were the first to market it in Europe. It represents 2mm to the foot (1:148) in the UK. The initial quality mass production examples for the UK were from Graham Farish and Hornby/Minitrix.

You can get smaller still today, with Z (track gauge 6.5mm) and T (track gauge 3mm) scales.

It is useful to work out the length of a full train that you would like to operate on your layout. Multiply the longest vehicle lengths for the desired number of carriages, tankers, etc., add in the locomotive and then calculate whether you would be able to run them and occupy a platform or siding. Here, Lionheart in O, Airfix Railways in OO and Graham Farish in N show the relative lengths involved for a suburban coach. Do not forget coupling gaps, which are often missed out of calculations.

Are not both TPOs true scale? The problem is their relationship to track width. That on the left is a Jouef 3.5mm HO scale sold under the Playcraft label in the 1970s. On the right, Hornby 4mm OO scale. The inability to mix and match on a layout meant that any ingress to the UK market by HO manufacturers had to be with a wide product range, something that never happened.

The author's trusty Land Rover showcases The Priory, a 2mm scale N gauge club vignette kindly donated to the club and currently being expanded. It demonstrates that a whole neighbourhood can be put into a display of just 26 x 18in (66 x 46cm).

The main station of Edwardian Woodcroft. All track and turnouts have been built by hand, the builders using jigs to maintain the gauge. Overall, the aspect ratio of the track width feels right to the eye of someone used to British railway formations. (*MDMRC*)

This section had extensive damage from scaffolding poles smashed through the baseboard, fortunately missing the track itself. A challenge has been to weather new scenic material so that it blends in with the older materials used. (*MDMRC*)

Restored layout, as seen at the NEC Warley Show in 2019. At the end of the cattle dock extensive damage led to a baseboard repair section being let in and blended to match. (*MDMRC*)

Layouts made with these can truly exist on a coffee tabletop or be carried in a briefcase.

Specialisms also exist within each scale. For example, in the OO area there exists the 18mm or EM track gauge for 4mm scale, regarded as a more correct ratio (see the Club's Woodcroft layout images following). More accurate still is P4/Scalefour, which uses an 18.83mm track gauge in the same scale.

Track Types and Standards

As with scale and gauge, the hobby is peppered with different products and standards where trackwork is concerned. The types of track available off the shelf vary in realism, robustness and compatibility with certain types of wheels. For the more advanced modeller there are individual components on sale so that track chairs, rail type and sleepers can all be varied to represent specific prototypes rather than use the generic offerings.

In most gauges you also have two options of ready to run track formations. With 'set' track, the curves, standard straight lengths and points/turnouts all have the ability to generally fit together with a minimum of issues and you can follow example plans which give a recipe list of the components required. Such track also comes in a boxed 'train set' where you get a circuit and rolling stock to start a layout. With flexible (flexi-) track you lose the geometry definitions and replace them with your own, enabling you to get closer to the prototype. You can normally mix and match the different types as desired, as long as you ensure the rail grade sizes are identical.

In Europe, N gauge can have code 55 or code 80 track, where the number represents the height of the rail top above the sleeper. As 55 thousandths of an inch is smaller than 80 thousandths of an inch, code 55 is closer to 'real' scale for the track cross section. There is the possibility of some crossover between sourcing manufacturers and the codes. For example Peco and Arnold can be linked with a little cutting of sleepers and the same track connectors are used at the base of the rail.

Care should be taken with older stock (e.g. Triang) with thicker wheel flanges which will have difficulty even on standard SL 100 track as the flanges will not pass through the plastic guide rails on points and jump them, leading to jerky movements, or in the worst circumstances locomotives come to a complete standstill causing the stock behind to derail.

If desired, especially in the smaller scales, you can buy track that has a simulated pre-ballasted base, such as that from Kato or Fleischmann. This removes the finishing challenges that can occur when trying to apply fine chippings and glue to create ballast. Their granular 'flow' does not scale well and it can be frustrating getting things into the correct place.

Model railway track examples showing varying detail and manufacture technique over time. L–R:
- N gauge Peco Streamline nickel silver track code 55 rail.
- OO gauge Peco Streamline nickel silver track SL100 code 75 rail.
- OO gauge Hornby/Triang early steel track (Austrian production).
- OO gauge Hornby Dublo three rail track produced in the late 1930s to the early 1960s. The live pickup is in the middle and the rolling stock wheels return the circuit. This is early track as it has a rounded connector.
- Gauge L700BH code 124 Bullhead track from Peco.
- Gauge 'coarse scale' from Hornby for tinplate clockwork and early electric train sets (if with a third central rail). Less a model, more a toy, but everything was in the eye of the beholder.

When you get to HO/OO you may think the track is generally compatible between European and British scales because what differs is the rolling stock size above the rail level. But since codes 100, 83 and 75 exist and the sleeper spacing and track attachment types all differ, it becomes a case of buyer beware.

	Gauge	Scale	Ratio	Useful information
	T 3mm	0.64mm	1:450	Available as ready to run introduced by KK Eishindo of Japan in 2006. Based on Japanese 3ft 6in gauge. www.tgauge.co.uk
	Z 6mm	1.40mm	1:220	Much European outline and a growing UK prototype base being produced.
	N 9mm	1.90mm	1:160	Large selection of standard N gauge. www.ngaugesociety.com or for 2mm finescale option www.2mm.org.uk
	TT TT3 12mm 13.5mm	2.50mm 3.00mm	1:120 1:101	There are three interest areas all covered by www.3mmsociety.org.uk: TT UK outline, TT3 European outline, 3mm finescale.
	HO	16.5mm	1:87	There is limited British prototype production such as that by Jouef, covered by the group www.british-ho.com. Other good support tends to be associated with societies representing the countries being modelled. Magazines such as *Continental Modeller* cover the hobby well in this area.
	OO	16.5mm	1:76	For the UK this is the largest range of products and has the best support from the major manufacturers for ready to run sets and items, scenic kits and associated hobby publications. www.doubleogauge.com For older Hornby Dublo tinplate and diecast, including spares and repairs, HRCA.net (Hornby Railway Collectors Association).
	EM	18.0mm	1:76	The EM Association www.emgs.org, covering 18mm topics.
	P4	18.83mm	1:76	P4/Scalefour, www.scalefour.org, for precise gauge within the scale.

	S 7/8in	3/16in	1:64	S scale is a mainly scratch built scale in imperial measurements. Originally it was an American toy standard scale in the early twentieth century, but has moved since then to a more precise scale/gauge definition. In the UK there are kits and scratch build assistance from www.s-scale.org.uk.
	O 32mm	7mm	1:43	UK outline standards championed by the gauge O Guild. In recent years the scale has seen a resurgence and more ready to run options have been made available due to modern production and design techniques making this cost effective. www.gaugeoguild.com European runs on same track dimension but the body ratios differ. North American is 1:48 scale NMRA (National Model Railroad Association) standards. Scale 7 exists as a precise 33mm gauge option. www.scaleseven.org.uk
	G 45mm	-	1:20– 1:29	Effectively a garden scale narrow gauge. Robust trackwork and rolling stock with a wide variety of mainly European options. Can run with live steam or electric. www.g-scale-society.co.uk

Narrow Gauge

Having touched upon scales we should also consider mixed or narrow gauge as space saver solutions.

Conceptually, you can fit more in by selecting narrow gauge track and either incorporating it into a standard gauge layout as a feeder operation or creating a purely narrow gauge setup, as exists in many places worldwide in many forms, Welsh quarry lines being a good example.

If modelling the USA, the narrow gauge locomotives can actually be articulated and approach the size of main line examples. Alternatively, the diminutive Welsh quarry 0-4-0 Hunslet half cab saddle tanks take things back the opposite way and you can fit more trucks/carriages in as a result.

A number of options exist. For example, HOn3 American outline is used to model the historic Denver and Rio Grande Western's Colorado system. For British outline there is OO9 (or HOe) which approximates to a 2ft 3in prototype, a scale and gauge combination of 4mm scale and 9mm (0.354in) gauge track with scale/wider sleeper spacings. This is catered for in the UK by the 009 Society.

If modelling in 7mm or O gauge narrow gauge the tracks are called On30 tracks. They are the same gauge as HO/OO track. However, depending on which country you pull the rolling stock from, you will get a varied scale definition. From the USA it will be 1:48 scale,

whereas from Europe 1:45 and from the UK 1:43.5 – so it is difficult to do any mix and match. Likewise, trackside buildings and accessories need to be consistently sourced from the same country.

To further confuse the situation, some choose to use O gauge track and scale up to 1:32 for the rolling stock. This takes advantage of another source of accessory models but really is for the dedicated/experienced modeller.

Above: Mixed gauge exchange sidings demonstrate the comparative sizes of a Union Pacific 'Big Boy' and a Denver and Rio Grande 'Challenger' locomotive. (*Alan Hancock*)

Right: Stepping down from USA to UK outline: effectively the same scale, but a different gauge, showing that you can choose from a wide selection of options. (*Alan Hancock*)

3

Planning Your Layout

Mix and match. If you search hard enough you can find just about any prototype for running stock on a line of your choice. Here is the Paddington main line in October 1977 looking towards the Southall water tower in West London. An unidentified Class 25 with match trucks for London Underground couplings pulls a nine-car rake of red liveried 1938 Tube stock. This is probably heading to Bird's Yard at Long Marston for scrapping, following component stripping performed at Neasden Depot. Note the 'LH' on the distant tower, a leading mark to the London Heathrow lesser used cross runways that existed in the pre ILS guidance days. (*Derek Mulquin/GWRPG*)

Planning your layout to ensure a successful conclusion involves a number of blended skills if you wish to get something that will satisfy and meet your end requirements. We will cover some key planning activities, the importance of which vary according to your own innate skills and ability to expand them and also whether you actually want to do so.

You may decide on the equivalent of a preserved railway based on 'Anysuch Junction' where all your favourites can appear. You can drop any prototype research or working out how to distil a specific scenario into available space. You can even dispense with making your own baseboard. But you will need to lay some track, do some wiring and integrate some scenery as a minimum, even if this one is for the kids and your own layout will come later.

A recent members' discussion covered loft clearances of children's layouts constructed over time and being passed on now that they have their own homes and families. Think whether they would actually continue in the hobby themselves and over time how much the quality and technology of the products have moved on.

Here are four key points that move your original decisions into the active phase.

1. **Determination.** What am I doing? Gauge, scale, location, historical age. Research into prototypes; compromises to be made for space; availability and cost.
2. **Resource utilisation.** Where will it eventually live? How easy it is to set up and use? Where are you going to do the messy work of construction?
3. **Planning.** Pre-plan the track, wiring and scenic requirements before committing to anything.
4. **Actualisation.** How much time and dedication do I have? Chances are you need to loop back to decision 1 and go through it all several times until you really have it set in stone. Then you are ready to make your final plan and execute it.

The planning phase can be undertaken in a number of ways. As a bare minimum you are aiming at a track layout that fits your available space and the reverse – a board configuration that will take the track and any extra scenic areas required without too many compromises.

From all this you will be able to determine the usability, whether it will be interesting to build and operate, a list of track and components to purchase or consume from storage and a list of materials to make the boards (or a size of board to buy). You may wish to take things deeper before committing and also plan the electrical schematics. Some people prefer to do this on a discovery basis later on.

You can design using plain or graph paper, cardboard cutouts, any spare 'ready to run' track or using computer software (CAD). There are also options such as the Hornby trackmat and Peco layout books. It all depends on where your skills and interests lie and each has its place.

Personal hobbies are very much a 'broad church' covering a large number of variations and demands on space. For example, here, where layout construction shares space in a garage. A 1968 Land Rover makes a very useful tool stand and wood store during the construction phase. Little did the Solihull designers of yesteryear realise just how their SWB pickup would be abused!

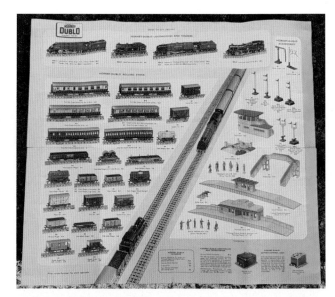

The 1950s Hornby Dublo catalogue was really just a single page – a train set was just that, a toy and not expected to be extended far.

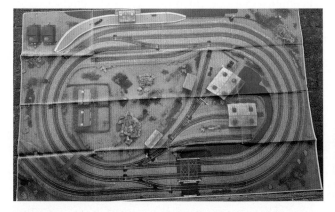

Nowadays many sets come with a durable trackmat on which you can lay the track each time the set is retrieved for use.

You also need to be aware of the limitations imposed by your rolling stock. The same locomotive offering from two different vendors has been seen to have radically different turning circles due to the methods used in chassis compensation. Research as much as possible and if you have already purchased, always dry run before fixing your track permanently.

Examples of computer aided design (CAD) products

Company	Web address	Description
3d Plan It	https://www.trackplanning.com/index.htm	A 3D track planning package. You can draw everything from the room you're in to the trains you're running. A demo version is available for free download but you will be limited to 100 objects and there will be no 'save' facility.
AnyRail	https://www.anyrail.com/en	AnyRail is probably the easiest to use model railway design tool around. It's also entirely independent, so you can build with almost any track. Enjoy designing your layout – AnyRail ensures everything fits. AnyRail enables you to rocket through the planning phase, or tinker to your heart's content – you don't have to be a computer expert to produce successful designs. You can print out to any scale but may need a lot of paper!
Cadrail	http://www.sandiasoftware.com/	There is a free download available which allows you to build a layout of up to 60 pieces. 3D views are possible using this software.
Railmodeller	https://www.railmodeller.com/home-railmodeller.html	The only drawing programme we have found to our knowledge that runs on Macs. There is a free trial version available.
SCARM	http://www.scarm.info/index.php	SCARM stands for Simple Computer Aided Railway Modeller – software for easy and precise design of model train layouts and railroad track plans.
Templot	http://www.templot.com	Free precision track design for model railways by Martin Wynne. This is very different from layout design software as it is primarily a workshop tool for modellers who want to build their own precision track.
Winrail	https://www.winrail.com	For designing and drawing model railway layouts. A free trial version is available via the downloads page.
XTrackCad	http://xtrkcad-fork.sourceforge.net/Wikka/HomePage	Free product. XTrackCAD is a CAD program for designing model railroad layouts. Using it, you can • design layouts in any scale and gauge • use the predefined libraries for many popular brands of turnouts to help you get started easily • add your own favourite components, • manipulate track, much as you would with flexitrack to modify, extend and join tracks and turnouts • test your design by running trains, including picking them up and moving them with the mouse. At any point you can print the design in a scale of your choice. When printed in 1:1 scale the printout can be used as a template for laying the track to build your dream layout.

The Sankey Viaduct of the Liverpool and Manchester Railway. Designed by George Stephenson and carrying much of the detailing of stone bridges and aqueducts of the previous century, such as the column bases. This nine-arch construction had to be wide enough to span the Sankey Brook and the accompanying canal carrying coal from the St Helens coalfield to the coast and with a minimum of 18.3m clearance – high enough to allow the masts of fully rigged coal boats to traverse. Today the major changes are the filling in of the canal in 2002 and the overhead pylon assembly of the 2015 electrification. When considering such a component on a model railway, imagine wooden noggins as uprights with a sturdy trackbed attached. Then, clothed with the desired finish, it will also need abutments and embankments, creating a dominant but imposing feature. (*Wikipedia Commons: Adam Lomax*)

The same viaduct, but this time shown in a contemporary painting from the publication Bury's *Coloured Views on the Liverpool and Manchester Railway* (1831). When thinking of constructions for a layout it is useful to blend research materials to help decide what to use. Early paintings, diagrams, architectural drawings and the like can give a good definition of what the constraints and requirements were. Real life sometimes differs in the execution undertaken by builders or by later conversions and repairs made. Even if you are not working on the concept of modelling a specific prototype, taking a source and bending it to your needs will result in a layout with a coherent look and feel. (*Wikipedia Commons*)

Market Obthorpe: A CAD Example

Club member Brian Norris coordinated the complex build of this O gauge layout using AnyRail as the basis. The sectional controls were defined along with the physical track layout on a grid representing the main baseboards. Because of space constraints only two boards could be erected in the club room at a time so careful planning was required.

Firstly, the general positioning was agreed and the same coordinates were mapped to the boards. Electric point and signal controls were to be by the MERG programmable board hubs so that also needed to be decided upon before physical tracklaying took place.

As can be seen below the general colourised plan included control sections and numbered points and signals. In the middle we see that a Gantt chart drove the project forwards. There are certain pinch points where specific skills are needed and critical paths where an activity cannot proceed until the previous one has been completed.

Below the Gantt chart there is a wiring diagram to determine the loading of the MERG board hub chips and their outline designations (See Chapter 7 on control panels).

Computerisation has largely replaced paper systems and enabled team communications by email.

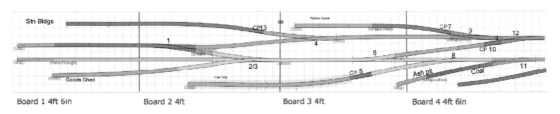

Board 1 4ft 6in   Board 2 4ft   Board 3 4ft   Board 4 4ft 6in

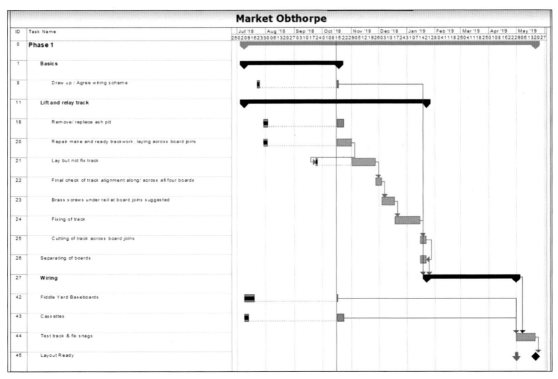

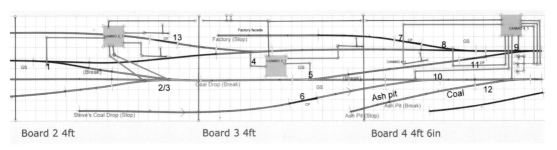

Board 2 4ft   Board 3 4ft   Board 4 4ft 6in

Severed Valley Railway: A Manual Plan Example

This Club member layout will appear in a number of places in this book as an example of a railway situated in a loft. While there have been several iterations over time in different houses, this version is planned and executed based on sixty years-plus of modelling experience. It demonstrates that you do not need to be a computer wizard to progress planning: the HB pencil, paper and a ruler still very much have their place.

It is possible to go by line of sight, placing rails down and moving them around until you are happy. It all depends on your personality and available time. Planning ahead for location, structure and wiring will make sure there are no rude shocks in future and that the general look and feel will the test of time. You are often

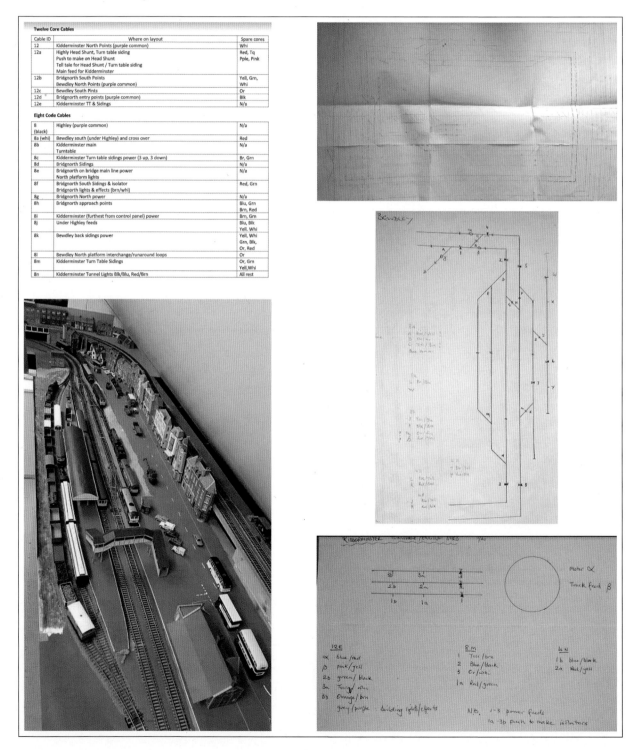

your own worst critic, so it is good to prevent issues and future annoyances by planning as much as you can and allowing for expansion should that be desired.

Ventnor, Isle of Wight: Scale Prototyping Example

Club member Graham Hobbs is a trained artist. He has the ability to realise complex prototypes by constructing an architect's model before commencing any construction. This is a useful technique to portray a complex scene in three dimensions before committing to actual construction.

His Ventnor Isle of Wight station model is of an imposing amphitheatre where the terminus station and goods yard complex was cut into chalk rock. This exited north into a single track tunnel mouth which acts as route to the fiddle yard. The actual station was built in 1866 within what was then an operating quarry.

The baseboard has to come apart into two sections and be portable, so is of a modular ply cutout framework with a polyurethane foam lower section and a thinner upper skin secured on wire fixings forming the cliffs, caves and hillsides.

The mock-up, based on 1:10,000 track plan, allowed the complex morphology to be worked out in miniature. This avoided nasty surprises during the actual board construction phase and ensured that the trackwork and buildings were correctly positioned and scaled.

Since some turnouts would need specialist construction, good accuracy was required in marking out on the layout itself.

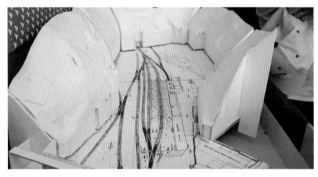

Above: Fitting neatly into a shoebox lid, the printed track plan of the quarry and station forms the core of the three-dimensional plan. (*Graham Hobbs*)

Below: The prototype in the days of British Railways, taken from the hillside above the tunnel mouth. Some of the caves can be seen on the right-hand wall. It is a quiet goods yard as services have been run down prior to eventual closure, but all major buildings are still present. Graham is making good use of photographic evidence to determine absolute positions for the years being modelled. (*Wiki Commons*)

Above and below: Looking towards the north of the station and the tunnel mouth in the chalk rock face on the mock-up and the actual baseboard construction. A number of caves were used for storage around the station and they form an interesting addition to the challenge of modelling this area.

The outline of buildings is being made in lightweight white card prior to committing to the actual bespoke building phase in heavier materials.

The board breaks in two, laterally east/west beyond the curved roof shed.

The upper farm field slope construction is the next major step in the build sequence.
(*Graham Hobbs*)

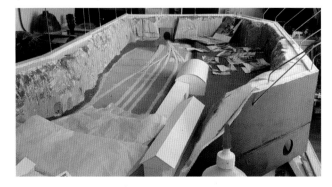

Storing a Portable Layout

If you have chosen the route of using demountable boards for your layout, thus allowing space to be freed up for other purposes, you need to think of the most efficient saving of space and also the ability to protect the layout when in storage.

You can build your own rack to receive each board for storage but must ensure the clearance is good enough for the scenery height on each board. If you observe the setup and breakdown of a model railway exhibition you will see a number of different techniques. The end aim is to fit into a car or trailer and not break anything in transit.

The most common approach is the use of end boards to attach as spacers and the use of existing bolt holes. The inner scenic faces of the boards are then opposed in a rigid format. To achieve this the two boards need to be of the same dimensions and the scenery permanently attached has to be designed to be clear of vertical conflict.

You can see from examples that there is some side access where a backscene board is not available to infill, but generally there is adequate protection.

Ensure your storage location is dry and flat, avoiding tension or warp over time and ideally covered with old sheets or blankets to prevent dust ingress. Domestic spider populations love to set up shop inside your town, village or station. Protective sheeting helps keep the critters out.

Right: Euston Square Gardens, OO gauge.

Below left: Cannons Cross, OO gauge.

Below centre: Butterwick, O gauge.

Below right: Woodcroft, EM gauge.

Turning the Corners

Unless you have just a simple end to end layout you will need to introduce curves in the trackwork, whether it is to negotiate from a scenic section around to a rearward fiddle yard or to follow the imposed geometry of a room in which the baseboard is installed. You will need to determine your minimum possible dimensions.

Model rolling stock is designed to have much tighter cornering ability than the real thing. Bogies rotate, couplings are wider spaced and locomotives have chassis compensation with flange alterations, to allow you to run on curves that would spell disaster on the real railway.

While there are minimum radii listed, if you are able to exceed this minimum, you will find both handling ability and aesthetics improved. If you are able to introduce the concept of an 'easement' on your curves to get a gentle transition, you will find that stock looks and handles much better. Even if you are generally using set track for the curve, the use of a flexitrack section to introduce the radius gradually will help. This facet used to demonstrate itself well with the old tabletop Hornby Dublo tinplate. All track was a fixed size, and a train would throw itself around the two radii of curves available. However, the larger curve was always the one where uncoupling, derailments or dramatic whole tinplate train turnovers were at a minimum. The lesson was learned to integrate the two sizes where possible and get an average return which worked well.

Where you have more that one track rounding a corner you will need to increase the track spacing. This is to allow for body overhang between vehicles on adjacent tracks. It is best achieved by varying the release point from straight to curve, starting with the inner track working outwards. Most important is the setting out of track before final fixing into place and testing vehicle clearances on tracks by running your longest vehicles against each other.

Adept modellers even attempt 'super elevation' by canting the trackbed angle, thus allowing faster travel, as with the prototype. When performed it can really carry the eye through a train's travel. For mere mortals, if flexitrack is used for a curve you can gently introduce the curvature before the full radius tightness is reached – you will see trains behave more prototypically as they do not 'throw' into the bend.

Overall, the radius of curves (and of turnouts as well) will depend on the style of layout desired. A quarry can have minimum sizes since everything is four-wheeled short wheelbase. A large mainline layout with concomitant train movements will need larger curves and wider spacing.

The following is a general guide to the minimum curve radii by scale as issued within the Club for planning a layout (although we do not yet model in all these scales, it is useful to have a standard).

- Z gauge radius 195mm.
- N gauge radius 240mm.
- HO/OO gauge radius 500 to 550mm.
- HOn3/OOn3 radius 380mm.
- O gauge radius 1280mm.
- G gauge 610mm to 1120mm.

In spite of the above, always test, ask online, ask at exhibitions. As noted, narrow gauge, for example, can vary from the Welsh narrow gauge saddle tanks to huge articulated locomotives from the USA. Your prototype, your modelling compromises and the limitations of available locomotives and stock wheelbases, wheel compensation and couplings all come into play.

Modern locomotives will have a radius restriction listed on the box and in the brochure if it exists. If you are buying second hand you will have to research any radius issues online, especially in the smaller scales where a small difference can result in a non-running locomotive on some or all of a layout.

4
Baseboard Construction

Baseboard construction is your own major engineering works, requiring planning and careful execution. Here, on 4 November 1962 is a bridge replacement at Worcester Park, Sutton, South West London. Excavations are by Caffin, a London civil engineering company founded in 1908, who are using a Ruston Bacyrus 22. Steelwork is from Butterley Works, Derby. Spoil transport is by Perkins-engined Ford Thames and Ford Trader from Greenham Ltd. The Austin Cambridge and Morris Oxford Farina saloons belonging to the senior engineers cap it all off. (*AND-M488-1 Online Transport Archive*)

Eventually the time will come when you decide that you have planned enough and need to get down to some physical baseboard construction. For some it will be a labour of love, for others a necessary evil to get out of the way before the 'real' modelling is done.

Model railway clubs have their share of character types, which means that ideally there is a person that enjoys each facet of the building process. However we are illustrating the build process for some real-world home layouts, where one person has to cover all the skills and it can initially seem daunting.

Firstly, ensuring you have the correct tools is sensible: there is a minimum without which the build process becomes difficult or inaccuracies creep in. As would be done at a club, do not indulge in 'make do and mend' with key tools. If you can replace the wonky set square and bent tenon saw inherited through five generations it is good to do so. The correct tool for the job that is sharp, true and unlikely to fail on you is a wise investment.

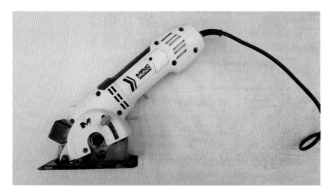

Small hand-held circular saw with a sprung surround guard for blade protection. This was a game changer for sheet material handling.

The basics

Must haves
- Sharp pencils
- Tape measure and ruler
- 90° set square (or modern saw which has 45° and 90°settings on the handle)
- Fine-toothed ripsaw and/or tenon saw
- Cramps for compressing and holding work when you run out of hands
- Some sort of hand drill with a selection of drill bits suitable for use on wood
- A decent selection of screws and nails, ideally new and of useful sizes for your plan
- Claw hammer and screwdrivers or screw bits

Should haves
- A breathing mask for dust
- Protective eyewear
- Work bench (fixed or portable)
- A professional long straight edge (or unwarped timber)
- A Dremel or mini drill
- A rail cutting jig
- An electric jigsaw for awkward cutting out
- One-hand G cramps
- Mitre block or mitre cutter
- A small circular saw for cutting sheet materials
- A first aid kit plus tweezers for the inevitable splinters

Compressive G cramps, allowing one hand operation to secure material. (Pedants please note: for our purposes a 'cramp' and a 'clamp' are essentially the same – 'cramp' tends to be used in woodworking to describe a device used to hold two or more pieces of wood together for as long as it takes for an adhesive to set, while 'clamp' is preferred in engineering.)

A trusty/rusty mitre saw assembly. Fairly cheap with a small-toothed blade and 10° gradations to the bed which allows for a number of tricks for baseboards (and the occasional household miracle as well).

Severed Valley Railway: An Unconverted Loft Layout

This experienced club member's home layout is in the insulated loft of his house. An essential asset is the apex insulation between the rafters which keeps the loft area stable from extremes of temperature and prevents ingress of blown dust.

Originally it had middle access from a loft hatch. Latterly it has been changed to walk-in access as the loft section is now entered from a room on the same level. The baseboards themselves are made from two repurposed table tennis tables, cut in half and used as four robust sections on timber framing.

Things ideally pre-prepared in such a layout location are decent flat flooring with access points for the lighting circuit of the floor below, dry lining and painting of the inner roof, and installation of decent ambient lighting,

House construction differs by age as to whether there are obstructing beams and diagonal or vertical posts in a loft, and similarly, insulating and dry-lining the loft to reduce temperature variations from freezing

to boiling can be difficult to perform. Track problems can occur, some plastics can warp or melt, plus it can be uncomfortable to be within the working area in times of extreme heat or cold. If in doubt refer to experts: you may line out a loft only to trap moisture and bring other issues through an ill-ventilated space.

With regards to the actual access and clearances the diagonal nature of the inner roof has to be taken into account. While a nice siding tucked behind the main line looks good on paper, the triangular cut-off of an unconverted space reduces headroom. Since this layout runs on two levels to provide a double pass for trains the cut-off is a real limitation on what seems on paper to be accessible and with an adequate loading gauge.

Right: Since the boarding is a substantial reclamation material, the depth of the layout into the slope of the roof was already dictated. As you can see, good lighting plus the white loft lining colour combines to give reduced shadow and a decent highlighting of the layout without recourse to other sources. The overall area is helped by having a gable end rather than a hipped roof.

Below: The key to rigidity here is frequent supporting members and legs to the floor as seen from the entrance end of the layout. It allows for a decent space for storage into the eaves of the roof as well. You don't want to lose the ability to stow articles away for a rainy day.

Innsdorf: Swiss Outline Spare Room Baseboard

Club member Rev. Mark Warwick had a dual task to perform when installing a new fixed layout. Firstly to be able to store an old OO exhibition layout, Kingsgate, flat and safe, secondly to have a new baseboard to produce a Swiss-based HOn narrow gauge layout. The technique used was to batten and cantilever supports from the wall directly at two levels, taking the board the length of the room, but not to run round the room itself, taking over all the space.

An important thing when fixing a layout into the walls of a house is to be aware of where any mains wiring could be behind the plaster. Use a detector to be sure that you are not about to blow the mains and consequently yourself across the room. With partition walls try to locate the uprights supporting the plasterboard

Above left, centre and above right: Three stages in construction: checking the mains, especially since so close to an outlet; drilling pilot holes for cantilever; constructing a braced bracket capable of taking lateral weight. (*Mark Warwick*)

Right: The lower level support complete and the old layout safely stowed to await a future restoration. (*Mark Warwick*)

Below left: Frame construction using screw-in blocks to secure the elements. (*Mark Warwick*)

Below right: The finished first board in situ and marked out with proposed running lines for the layout. (*Mark Warwick*)

as the strongest point – the cantilever can damage the wall if you place your weight on it.

Baseboards themselves can be of a basic construction and use heavy blockboard or MDF as desired since they are a fixture. In this case 1cm MDF and board framing are used, making use of plastic screw blocks similar to kitchen unit construction. When completed the structure is rigid and at an ideal height to work on when seated, while leaving enough space in the room in general to maintain a workbench for modelling and tall shelving for miscellaneous hobby accessories.

Butterwick: A Simple Extension Board for O gauge

Butterwick needed to grow from two detail boards and a fiddle yard to three detail boards with a longer station platform. It was developed for a limited storage and display space situation but this is no longer a key constraint. More stock is available for it and there is a personal desire to showcase it.

This meant that a new board had to be built to the same standards and measurements as the

Aerial view of Butterwick in two-board format. The tape measure shows where the existing board join is located. The opportunity will be taken to correct water damage from a storage mishap at the same time and therefore old and new paint finishes will match. Effectively a 4ft (1.2m) board will be dropped in here and everything extended.

Left: A long view from the fiddle yard giving a 12ft (3.6m) overall length to the existing short form layout. You also get a feel for the layout in 7mm O gauge – you cannot get a lot into the space. If this was in 2mm N gauge it could be a comprehensive main line station and loop. The requirement is to be able to fit this into an estate car and be able to breathe.

Below: The third board of the equation, the fiddle yard, is actually a flat board with trackwork emerging from the scenic detail and feeding into cassettes to remove stock. These have normal track stuck in place. Alternatively angled aluminium or steel bars could have been used to make a more rigid cassette as these may warp when lifted. Another project will make a traverser at this junction between boards.

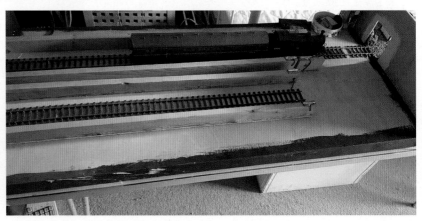

original, so that it could run in two- or three-board format as needed. Beware – size can still differ according to supplier.

Fortunately the original was constructed from new wood as opposed to reclaimed, so the new board used standard off-the-shelf sizes. Track and wiring had to be added and these are covered in later chapters.

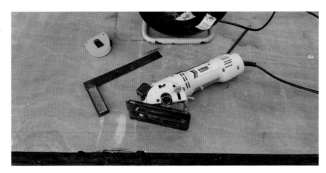

The weapon of choice for cutting 5mm ply is a craft circular saw. It has a spring-loaded shield and alternate choices of fine or coarse tooth blades. The speed of such a saw is normally enough to ensure that a cut is clean in ply, without splinters that would come from ripsaw cutting.

The carpenter's adage of 'measure twice cut once' holds true in any woodworking project. So sizes are double checked and the cut positions are marked out with a set square.

With power tools, ensure the wood is cramped or weighted in place to avoid slippage (in this case a handy passing wife stood on it). Also you need to ensure that any blade exposure underneath is not aiming at a leg, finger or wire.

Using the old faithful mitre cutter in 90° mode to ensure a correctly square cut for corners. With an intermediate board it has to maintain the correct profile to match the originals. They were previously measured to confirm 'squareness' and were still in line.

Close up of finished cut on the three-ply. Splinters from veneers are very nasty. Usually composed of hard, brittle wood they can break off under the skin causing infection, so some sanding or filing is still needed afterwards.

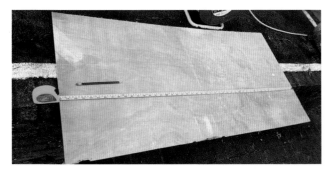

When using power tools please be aware that stability is required for safety, so a good work bench or table is needed. Here advantage was taken of a solid wheelchair access facility on the house as a workplace.

A trick for nailing: invert the nail and strike the point with the hammer. A blunt nail will break fibres rather than part them, thus avoiding any splitting of wood grain that could occur, especially if nailing close to the edge.

Above: 'Belt and braces'. This is a portable layout so a degree of stress will be encountered. PVA or specialist wood glue was used in addition to dovetailing the nailing (alternate diagonals).

Below: Finished glued and screwed corner, neat and strong, supporting the end timber which will be subjected to horizontal forces when bolted to the next board.

Above: Holes were drilled to pilot wood screws – again this is to avoid the wood splitting. Then a countersink was milled in order to bed the shoulder of the screwhead to surface level. It is neater, prevents splitting and where faces are to abut, a flat screwhead is required. If you lack a countersink, try a larger gauge drill bit running anticlockwise to abrade the screw head slot shoulder.

The finished board ready to offer up. It has two struts reinforcing it underneath preventing any flex of the thin plywood. While these would be stronger end on, they are presented on their sides to allow wiring to pass over without drilling holes. This is for the eventuality that a display is based on a school tabletop rather than on legs.

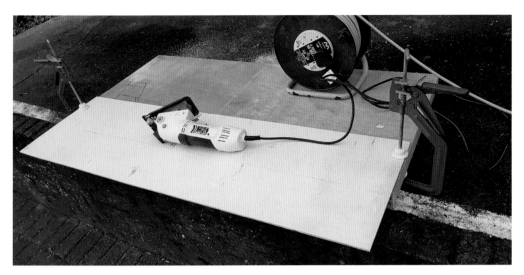

Above: Cutting the scenic backboard is a repeat of before, with a circular saw. If you are running out of board depth to cut, try cramping it onto the already constructed board to extend your safe area. You can then weight or secure the board itself to keep everything safe.

Below left: Offering up the new board into the gap. This is a dry run with track for testing joints and clearances, aiding planning for how the scenic area will be delivered in actuality. There is always room for inspiration and mission creep until the last minute. There was to have been a small overbridge with a footpath. This has now become a water mill leat going under the track and platform which requires more scenic skills and draws the eye.

Below centre: The position of the proposed watermill leat was drawn allowing a straight cut by circular saw and ensuring it did not foul the supporting member underneath. It also opened up under the turnout to allow easy point motor attachment.

Below right: The station platform is being created, final stock clearances determined, and the position of the point and solenoid motor being 'snagged' for the engine shed spur. The tracklaying example continues in a later chapter.

North Cape, Kimberley: A Club Experimental Panorama Baseboard

The proposal for this Club project was defined as follows.

1. We need something a little different that can take advantage of a less conventional approach; African outline in the UK is rare and we can showcase it.
2. Conceptually the track and trains are to become a part of a panoramic artwork set as a landscape letterbox.
3. Modules must be of an open-side box form without supporting front columns. No obstructions to the letterbox view between modules.
4. Display location light lux level must be controlled as much as possible to allow our own ambient light sources.
5. We wish to have both moving rail and roadway, thus requiring an embankment with road / river bridges.
6. The box form of each module has to be transportable, so lightweight and strong. Eco-friendly, aim for minimal waste of materials.
7. The layout has to be at a slightly higher eyeline than normal models as it is direct view and will contain two rows of LED lighting. A front top light strip will exist for direct strong sunlight. This will need to be dimmable to allow a light show to take place. Diagonally opposite at the scenic base at the back of the module, cut out hills will hide a full colour LED strip. This is to allow African sunsets to be emulated, projecting up the sky and cloudscape painted at the rear.

The overall idea was that running trains of a long consist would be largely silhouetted against chosen spectrum colours of skyline behind trees and other features.

Above: What triggers the decision for a layout? In this case a donation of a twelve-coach SAR (South African Railways) Blue Train with three Vulcan electric locomotives in HO. These rather rare beasts required some tidying and new overhead pickup pantographs. As a Club this was all new territory for us. As an artistic statement, think of a savannah semi-desert display with a full length train running through a sunset.

Opposite above: Initial brief – project line drawing representing the concept. Thoughts on eyelines and height of legs for the modules. It had to be very stable throughout the length of the layout. For disability access the higher eyeline still needed to be within the range of a seated person. The decision was made to construct from 9mm sheet ply and tesselate the cutting measurements and shapes to allow for minimal wastage/cost. With the onset of the Covid-19 lockdowns and distancing it had to be able to be built at home by a Club member.

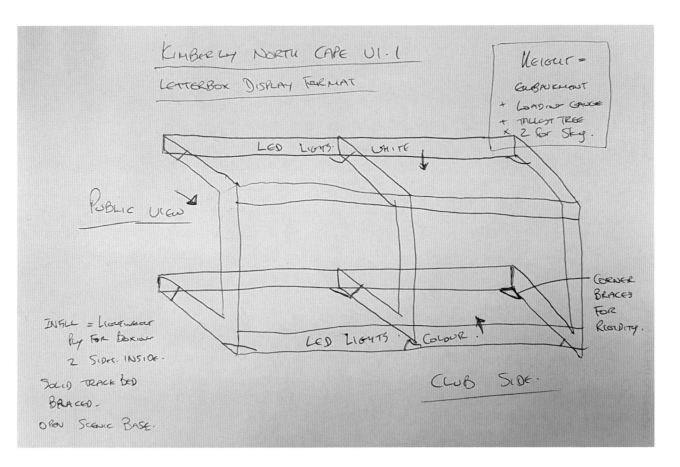

KIMBERLEY NORTH CAPE V1·1

LETTERBOX DISPLAY FORMAT

HEIGHT =
EMBANKMENT
+ LOADING GAUGE
+ TALLEST TREE
× 2 for Sky.

LED LIGHTS. WHITE

PUBLIC VIEW

CORNER
BRACES
FOR
RIGIDITY.

INFILL = Lightweight
Ply for Exterior
2 SIDES. INSIDE.
SOLID TRACK BED
BRACED.
OPEN SCENIC BASE.

LED LIGHTS. COLOUR.

CLUB SIDE.

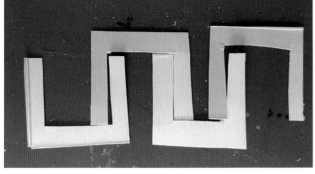

Left: Playing around with cardboard cutouts. Big industry would use CadCam but this suffices for the amateur.

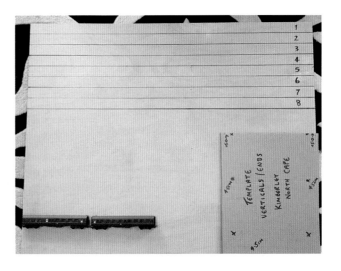

Right: Once the general layout of cutting was decided a template was made of triple wall cardboard for the C section to allow for consistent marking on these and future boards.

Materials were purchased to build two modules. Thick ply sheet 9mm x 1220mm x 91.5mm (4ft x 3ft) was deemed strong but lightweight and could be screwed/nailed securely. We used 25mm screws and 35mm oval nails for corner lapping. It was decided that just the two C sections were needed rather than the three planned, which allowed it to remain within the single sheet for cutting. The use of scale cardboard roughs of components helped with this decision before marking out.

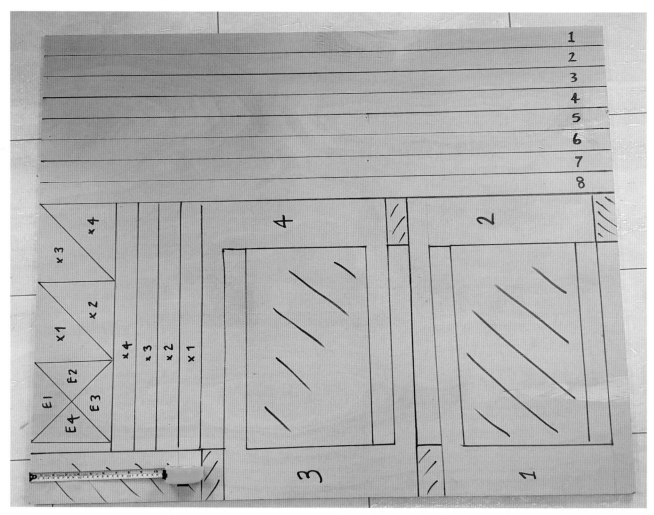

Above: The cutting sheet marked out onto the 9mm ply by using an end form C section template, plus measured spars and braces to provide for two modular baseboards. End pieces 1/2/3/4 would have locating studs and bolt holes both top and bottom to maintain rigidity throughout the length of the layout.

Below: Cutting was mainly performed using a hand-held circular saw to keep a straight line and reduce splintering of the plywood surface (something that a ripsaw or jigsaw produces when going across the grain). Finishing of corners was done with a fine-tooth jigsaw. This all produced a kit of parts to construct.

It was decided that the centre C section could be dispensed with as rigidity would return with sheet materials later. However, the additional pressures put on 9mm thickness endcaps could result in material failure when bolting adjoining boards together, so supporting 25mm x 50mm PSE timber was cut to size.

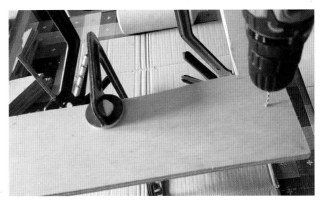

Because of the extra support layer, wood glue was applied, then timber cramped into place allowing adjustment. It was then inverted to allow for pilot hole drilling ready for 25mm screws to be inserted through the ply.

The pilot holes were then countersunk to allow a smooth surface after screwing. This is where boards join together, so as flat a surface as possible is needed to avoid distortion and gaps of trackbed junction.

Finally, the four long members were applied. Because they were made from 9mm ply the strongest join was through glue and 35mm oval nails. Remember to lightly tap the ends of nails with a hammer to make them blunt – they then punch into the wood, breaking rather than splitting the grain.

Long members attached and beginning to take shape. In this form there is torsional flex in the baseboard module despite corner bracing on the base, but this is removed in the next step.

Above: A module in completed state. Note that the top section is only partially infilled. A decision will be made later on as to what lightweight materials are best to black out the gap, in a discovery testing process. For now, building the trackbed and infilling scenery needs greater access than the end product will, so the gap is of benefit. The use of 5mm plywood on the scenic backing and fixed panel at the top acts as a lightweight 'I' beam. We needed to avoid twisting of the third form and this brings in the desired rigidity to the construction. It also demonstrates that the front viewing concept and downwards daytime bright LED lighting will be viable and not just something on a plan that fails in reality.

Below: Two completed modules offered up and cramped together on temporary legs. Mockups and testing are good for morale boosting and restoring confidence. Here it serves multiple purposes. Two lines are required on the embankment and the distance from the back of the board needs to be estimated to ensure there is adequate space for forced perspective hills. So here is a Blue Train set up on the base of what will be the embankment riser. The actual trackbed will be created 10cm higher than this. Two modules together also give an idea of the panoramic properties of the construction. At this point detailed scenic planning can commence as the track line becomes a fixed definition.

Above: The final drilling for the locator bolts between boards. Experimentation showed that despite the desire to prevent twist, some 'give' is useful at the top corners of the C section. Therefore, a single central bolt hole was drilled. The hole at the front (lower) should be singular, but despite taking great care this hole was initially drilled and produced metal swarf. We had forgotten to check the location of the nails and screws on the faceplate. So, with egg on face and a nice keen drill bit somewhat blunted, a second hole was drilled. Two bolts pass through the lower spar of the C section as the track needs to maintain relative position over the board joint. A pair of metal locating dowels (pattern makers' dowels) will also be added. Hint: as shown, when drilling fully through wood, use some scrap cramped on the other side to avoid the splintering of that face, especially if ply is used.

Below: The frontage was finished by squaring off with a sheet of ply. Next a coat of primer was added to the scenic backboard and this phase of the project could now be deemed complete. Next steps: the location of the lighting rig on opposite diagonals, top front and base rear and testing over joins. Three-dimensional printed retainers for the LED strips will be utilised using a Club design.

Measuring out of the roadway over both boards will be needed to incorporate the Faller HO 1:87 follow-the-wire system and the embankment will then be constructed with access bridges positioned to allow the road to feed moving cars back in the opposite direction. The track will then be tested for consistent level and associated electrical continuity.

This project will be continued in later chapters to show the type of activity undertaken. While the overall project seems complex, it breaks down into smaller logical segments. The only Club downside is the discovery that in real life we get no elephants in the river, however the Karoo National Park has large numbers of mountain zebra to compensate us.

Euston Station: Flat Board and Inserts

The Club's own London Euston Station layout uses one of the more difficult approaches to board building and is in standard 4mm OO scale.

The main section of this 100sq ft (9.3sq m) board is devoted to a mid-Victorian diorama of the Euston Arch and surrounding roads, buildings and parkland. As such what is normally the rail level is actually the platform top and road level.

When introducing the running lines to the rear of the station we had to adopt a 'cut slot and drop in' approach where each track section is below the natural baseboard level. It is only when the end of the platforms is reached that a 'natural' reversion can be made.

The boards for buildings have their own triple set of balancing legs forming a centre main board, then end legs for satellite boards. As a cohesive whole it becomes extremely stable and can support a great weight of constructions placed above, notably hotels and the Euston Great Hall.

The actual weight of the track-bearing boards is greater than normal as there is much supporting wood to drop the track level down. However it is rigid in nature and not deemed excessive.

For the purposes of transportation, the flat boards are easy to place and strap into a trailer as the track is protected within a board itself and the diorama buildings travel in their own separate boxes.

Euston Station as seen from the southern vista of Euston Grove. The two boards for Euston Square Gardens parkland locate as an independent add on, bolted to the front of the central three boards which have angled supports to their legs for rigidity. Beyond this, behind the arch and the station courtyard, baseboards then link caterpillar-style with single braced legs to a board end, taking advantage of the central rigidity. The weight of the LNWR cast iron sign when mounted on hooks to the front legs acts as an anchor, so if there is an accidental bump in exhibition the boards do not move at all. Overall, the station is modelled from Euston Road, proceeding north to Drummond Street via villas and hotels, through the admin buildings and Great Hall, proceeding to the first road bridge crossing at Camden Bank and the Railway Clearing House buildings, thus forming a substantial display. During construction runs it occupies an extended bay of a double garage as it is too large for the clubhouse. Therefore, available total space need not be a limiting factor if your end intent is public display. Winnie the black cat looks on bemused.

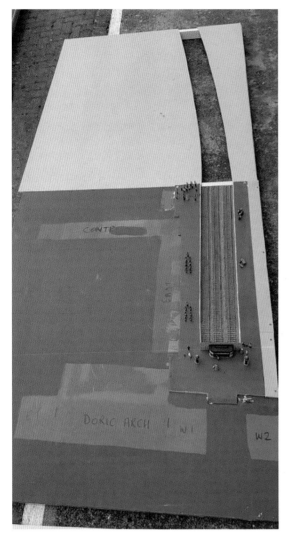

Above left: The flat board of the main station frontage was the first to have tracks let in. This marked the original 1838 Euston position. This is the only one to have above-level details and as such also required a shield to be created that could be bolted over the top during transportation and storage.

Above right: The Grand Hall board has the slot cut out for platforms 4 and 5 of the extended station. The triple line leading out to the station throat was the longest and normally for arrivals. As you can see, the normal supporting slats could not be added as they would obstruct the dropped trackbed. The top of all boards is 6mm MDF, heavier than ply. All boards have frame and hidden painting to stabilise in the event of weather extremes.

Working from one of the Victorian maps of the station it was seen that a triple carriage turntable still existed in 1875. A Triang model of an early carriage was used for scaling and geometry of the turntable position and the appropriate area was cut out of the board top.

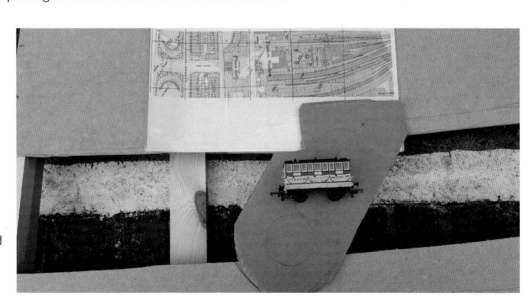

The Euston diorama is a good demonstration of the enjoyment of following an exact prototype, but also the constraints and problems that come from the need to compromise. One unexpected reward was in the results of the research. When you go deep and pull information from multiple sources, specialist publications, images, maps, plans, census returns, Hansard proceedings of Parliament, you begin to build a backstory as to 'why' something exists, filling in missing parts with reasoned arguments.

All buildings are demountable from the baseboard and due to their size need bespoke storage boxes made for them, an extra task not really foreseen. They also take up an appreciable volume for storage purposes so the boxes have to be strong enough to allow for stacking.

The boards have to be very sturdy to take the upper weight. Because the buildings came first, introducing the physical tracks as an afterthought led to an innovative approach by dropping them to be encapsulated within the baseboard structure and thus allowing them to be protected both in store and in transit.

Above: Once the primary platform area was cut it was used against plan for virtual positioning of other platforms.

Below left: Fillets of wood were adhered to the platform underside to drop the trackbed to the required depth, then 5mm ply was used to form the trackbed.

Below right: Finally, a top layer of MDF was added for the platform tops, and painted. As can be seen here the track level is naturally protected for transit and any above-the-board details can be boxed separately and positioned as required.

Right: Alternative views of the connection of the Great Hall and Main Station boards being made by cramping end timbers together. A pair of legs would also be bolted here, adding to the join strength. It can be seen that the simpler board is of a more traditional construction but with steels screwed to it to keep rigidity where the straight platform slot exists.

Below left: The Great Hall board offered up and connected with track on cork and in position. A train of four- and six-wheel LNWR coaching stock is being tested.

Below right: Growth continues, although only the east of the station is being modelled (the west is cutaway buildings). There are seventeen lines present on the next board heading to the complexity of the station throat and a fiddle yard where the steep gradient of Camden Bank would be in reality.

Fixed Layouts: Access Methods

A challenge for a fixed layout, especially of the circuit type, is how you get into the middle to access it and operate/rescue trains with problems.

If you are in the eaves of an unconverted house roof, think of a proper attached ladder as a bare minimum for access. This will give you a degree of safety although it is not ideal. If you emerge into the middle of your layout, so much the better, but ensure that you cannot accidentally step into the open void. Sounds sensible, but when you are away with your creative muse, simple things often get forgotten.

If you have a doorway to contend with you also need to think about emergency access. Most rooms such as a spare bedroom or box room will have an inwards-opening door. Your working railway would obstruct a closed door and prevent rapid access should a medical emergency occur. Think of reversing the door swing into the public area, or if fire precautions allow, using a space saver such as a concertina folding door.

While the easiest method is to just allow a duck-under you need to remember several things. You and others accessing the layout may not always be as nimble as today, and getting on your hands and knees is not always the most convenient method, although it does lift the requirement for wiring a demountable section. Ensure you pad the edges and cover any exposed nail and screwheads – the top of your head will thank you.

To allow a gangway without needing contortion there are several methods that can be undertaken. You can opt for a fully demountable section, ideally without much complexity or scenic material to damage, or a

Club member Peter Creigh's shed-based GWR layout has doorway with a lift out section between boards. Electrical connections are from phosphor bronze resting strip at the end docking points. (*Peter Creigh*)

Rather than just a practical bridging section it was decided to make a scenic feature of the requirement by detailing the link and multi-layering it to become a river and bridge section. (*Peter Creigh*)

River and bridge detailing were added, and the section kept lightweight but strong enough to hold two operating express trains at the same time. (*Peter Creigh*)

Access door closed, showing the finished link as a photogenic asset out of a necessity. King Class 6004 *King George III* at the head of a West Country express. (*Peter Creigh*)

lift-up section rather like a pub bar (think Del Boy in *Only Fools and Horses*). It would need a small trick with hinges being raised off the board to avoid damaging joints.

For the experienced craftsman, a swing-out section based on a pivot point and a curved meeting surface on the receiving board would be a solution.

Above: The loft layout of a club member has a curved join section with a double hatch due to the dual layers of running line combined with the radius restrictions of the loft geometry. The image has a red line drawn delimiting the hinge and face sides of the upper hatchway.

Left: The drawbridge is open. All scenics are attached and of lightweight construction. Hinges are flush with platform level and therefore allow a full 90° opening without any restriction.

Below: The underside of the upper hatch. The track here requires permanent link wiring so that as soon as the hatch is lowered everything is ready to go.

Above: In order to cheat the eye, the lifting section has overlapping station platforms; similarly with a part of the hillside behind. If you can disguise the construction of a join with a variable edge, the scenery stands more chance of appearing contiguous. The tracks however need to stay on the join to avoid accidental damage.

Below: The lower display section which contains the second pass line is yet to be detailed. It will be lower relief scenery to avoid damage when it too is lifted and retained in place. The aim is to disguise the access point. If needed it can all still be ducked under as a crawl access, but this is avoided as much as possible.

Above: Club member Graham Hobbs' layout Greatford Crossing has a swing out access on a fixed pivot point along the lines of a half door. This is the hinged point at 90°.

Left: The same seen from above. Highly detailed scenery pulls the eye away from contact points.

Below: The opposite side has the board cut in the arc of the opening to allow a smooth transition.

Above left: A ledge to support the end and a bolt serve to fully secure the arc end of the bridge.

Above right: When closed, the curving connection is a well-hidden joint.

Left: Rather than a full lower door this is a supported hinged post and brace, thus having a lighter weight construction.

Below: Showing the full width of the swing bridge access in open position.

Butterwick: O Gauge Traverser Project

Butterwick, as was seen earlier, is a small branch line portrayal in 7mm O gauge. It was perceived that it lacked flexibility at the fiddle yard end of the layout when full exhibition display was configured.

The default set up is with a cartridge style reception for a train. This can then be lifted off or rotated ready to run back onto the scenic sections and into public view. Because single locomotives and railcars are an option to run onto scene, it was decided that inserting a small interrupt board before the fiddle yard is reached would be the ideal solution. The aim is to allow the storage of several locomotives and also have a through line to feed the cartridge system. This would reduce the 'hand of god' activity, also protecting expensive locomotives from being frequently lifted off the board during busy display times.

After research, a base design was made and a recipe of ingredients concocted. There were also a number of restrictions. There was the danger of topple, caused by heavy locomotives on the traverser plate taking the centre of balance outside the lightweight board dimensions, should travel be too far. The baseboard framing had to be deeper than the normal framing to allow for the depth of mechanism and for the travel of the traverser plate to fore and aft of the current boards.

The baseboard needed to be braced to maintain rigidity, but not have a full 'tray' underneath the plate. When operating at an exhibition the 'tray' often becomes home for odds and ends and the occasional cup of beverage with consequent risks.

An old fitted drawer mechanism with fixed sliders and a smooth ball-bearing race was sourced. This would effectively act as the traverser base. It would not be electronically powered, but depend on hand movement and bolting into position. Aluminium angle iron would be used in conjunction with small furniture bolts to locate the traverser at rail centre junctions. Isolating switches per storage line would be on the operator side of the traverser to allow a single specific line to be energised once lined up.

An ideal example was spotted at an exhibition and photographed after a chat with the operators. Exhibitions should never be forgotten as a good source of information gathering for the home modeller. The challenge was to make an end result as good as that witnessed.

Like many clubs we have projects wating in the wings. We currently have a medium-sized GNR branch layout called Market Obthorpe under construction and absorbing manpower resources. In the soft planning stage is a GWR O gauge layout of Newtown Abbot Factory, which could potentially have traversers off stage at either end as it would be locomotive-heavy in operation.

Image of the traverser of Durham Street layout as made by the Scarborough and District MRC. Having seen this working at exhibition and its stability in use, it was decided after a chat with the operators that this would be an ideal small layout addition. After photographing, the concept was put on the back burner.

The connecting fiddle yard cartridge system of Butterwick. Simple, robust and flexible.

A spare set of enclosed bearing race drawer runners from a redundant slow-close cabinet.

Timber for front frame is lower to allow hinges to extend beyond the frontage.

Side frame is double depth to allow for mechanism.

Carcase is assembled and runners are spaced below baseboard level so that when a repurposed shelf is put into place the surface level reached 'floats' above the board framing.

'iewed a ng th ru ni g l ne wood lk comp sit wod e shelf cut size ill go el w the baset ard fi sh ng ay r. The am is o pre ent ra he gh at th cor ct le l and llo v a s ooth p iage f t e t av rs It s t e w h of ou rai s, ith the storage lines to the rear to counterbalance the assembly when in use.

Broad baseboard now in place (this could have been blockboard or thick plywood as an alternative) and attached to the slides. Care has to be taken that the slides travel the required distance, have a stop point on them and are also exactly parallel.

Viewed from the operator side. At baseboard top level adding offcuts of the same plywood that was used elsewhere on the layout. This is to bring the rails up to a level datum with other boards while still allowing a smooth sliding motion.

Rails are now cut to size and the domestic push bolt locators are being offered up. These will correspond with holes drilled into metal plates on the other boards to progress and locate each line. Aluminium bolts were chosen to allow new securing holes to be drilled in them as the baseboard ply is too thin to screw into at the sides.

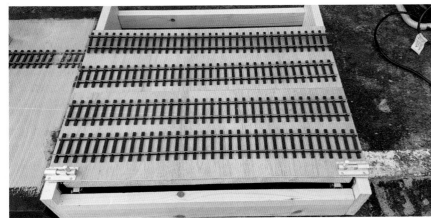

As with all projects in which you are exploring how to best do something, you find problems. It was discovered that the wood tried to twist itself out of true when the traverser plate was pushed. The remedy was to use corner plates on the underside to square the frame. These were nailed into place using annular ring nails which grip the wood fibres and prevent movement.

Dry run with loading on the traverser plate. Power wires will come from the live feeder line on the main baseboard and be interrupted by simple on/ off toggle switches to energise a line when required. The earth return will be wired as a common 'bus' feed between all lines. Wiring up is demonstrated in a later chapter.

Legs and Supports

If you are making a portable baseboard, you can wait until you are happy with the construction and then worry about how it will be kept at a decent level for operation. The reverse is true if you have a fixed setup in a room, garage or shed. With a bit of planning, you can make use of otherwise wasted space to store equipment, extra rolling stock, tools and household items.

Some consider making use of old kitchen installations, stripping out the countertop which will then become the baseboard level, storage

automatically coming with it. Alternatively, you can use racking systems to build the supports and the open shelving is then subsequently hidden with curtain material. Those built into a wall of a garage have drop legs that swing out as the board itself is lowered.

The portable layout has several options to choose from. DIY stores sell cutting or sawhorse bench legs in durable plastic or metal, and either is good for a mid-height setup. It is also possible to make your own trestle support legs in the same general shape and vary both the height and the method of securing to the layout to prevent accidental damage.

Clubs often take the opportunity of making legs that fold into the underside of a board. These tend to be asymmetrical to the board, attached to one end, allowing greater overall operating height to be attained.

Because of the extra manpower available when setting up at an exhibition, clubs will also consider larger detachable leg frames that slot into the board and are then braced and bolted into place.

Above: A shed-located baseboard which is built on steel frame rack shelving. It provides a consistent height throughout, is very stable with weight and gives great storage. Here garden weed supressing material is stapled to the front to blank off the shelves (shown looped over the layout itself to reveal the normally hidden view below).

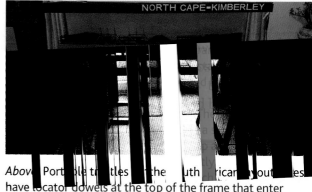

Above: Portable trestles on the South African layout have locator dowels at the top of the frame that enter into the baseboard corners, increasing stability, preventing slippage and linking the adjoining bolted boards.

Below: Basic trestles from PSE wood. The possibility of collapse under load is prevented by a simple tied cord. They are double hinged at the top and the legs are slightly angled inwards which greatly aids stability without making a trip hazard. Very much like a traditional sawhorse, but with lighter construction.

Commercial stands are a good option whether for working on a layout module or in series as a support. In common with the wooden trestle you need to be prepared to chock the feet to maintain a level surface.

An example showing the underboard view of a heavy leg frame locator on a new OO motive power depot layout that will appear in a subsequent publication. It does not need to be complex joinery but makes use of leg offcuts screwed and glued into place to ensure that lateral movement of legs is minimised before any bracing is added.

No matter how hard you try, each leg becomes a custom fit. When assembling, the position needs to be remembered and the end component clearly labelled to ensure it is always put back in the same position. We take rubber mallets to shows as the ambient humidity can affect fit and make disassembly challenging.

Plywood plate cross members are useful in that they both join and brace the legs in the correct position. Two plates like this per pair of legs at top and bottom, screwed and glued, hold the legs in the correct position without the need for a diagonal that thinner wood cross members would need. At the leg base, it is a good idea to use screw height adjusters to replace manual chocking when setting up.

5
Tracklaying

Laying a new configuration of track for the North London and the London Transport District terminus lines in Richmond Station, as captured on 1 February 1980. Crompton 33 002 is on light duty, seemingly ex-works. It oversees a second crane beside the camera position. To the north an unknown Class 73 electro diesel heads an engineers' rake past the signal box and the home of Continental Pioneer buses. Note the early roofbox RT resident there. A pair of 2 EPB slam door EMUs in solid corporate blue approach heading south on the through line. The inverted triangle denotes the end with the guard's compartment. Of interest to the modeller is that for once the professionals got it wrong in their design. A series of dead power sections were created where the surface stock tube trains would lose power successively; the jerking motion was accompanied by loss of internal lighting at the same time plunging commuters into darkness. Just to show, care in track must be accompanied by the same care in power provision. (*Author*)

Opposite above: Remember the humble siding where not only the sleepers rot – grounded ex-Pullman bodies built in Detroit/Derby in 1874. They were used as a bothy at Bradford Forster Square, seen here on 29 November 1972. The third-class baggage car nearest the camera was preserved by the Midland Railway Trust in 1975. (*Meredith 793-7 Online Transport Archive*)

Choose Your Track System Wisely

What track you choose depends on how ambitious you are. You can build your own from a variety of components. This way you can follow the track style of a historic company, the track chairs of a specific casting, bullhead, flat bottom, bridge rail or fishbelly track, turnouts that have a specific sleeper configuration. You will have to use a track gauge and plans or jigs for the more complex areas.

It is more likely that your choice is based on simplicity; you can use set track from a boxed set, expanding it, following a plan; you can choose flexible track or buy in professionally made track, such as a curved three-way point.

If you wish to avoid the fun of ballasting your permanent way you can buy pre-ballasted underlay or a track system that has it all there for you.

The stability and behaviour of the track system is only as good as the trackbed it is being laid upon. Ensure that gradients are moderate, and that lateral twisting of track is avoided to maintain good running and prevent derailments. The following pages show some tracklaying projects to demonstrate this activity.

N gauge pre-ballasted track system from Fleischmann.
HO/OO rubber ballast base set track sections from Roco.
Gaugemaster ballasted foam underlay and HO/OO Peco track.

The Witham OO exhibition layout built by Club member Martin Reynolds has a challenging divergence of gradients exiting the station. The requirement was to run six coaches or more by steam or diesel and ensure slipping was minimal. There are ways of increasing the tractive effort delivered to the rail top including scrupulously clean track, extra weighting or having powerful hidden magnets under the sleepers and locomotives. Martin was able to get around this challenge by having both lines diverge gradually, commencing from within the station platform. That on the left rises as that on the right falls away, resulting in a more dramatic effect than would otherwise be achieved.

North Cape, Kimberley : Club Layout, HO

When choosing the time for a layout there are always compromises on little things that a here-counters and purists will gracefully high on display, as shown in a publication. There are always ways of pulling the eye away from them and making a visual rather than a physical correction.

Here is the decision process we went through for this particular layout.

Our biggest issue was that the ready to run stock inherited was in HO scale and running on European standard gauge track, 4ft 8½in (1435mm) rather than the Cape gauge of 3ft 6in (1067mm) which exists in a number of African nations. It looks generally correct and while there is the ability to re-wheel and change the track used, it becomes expensive and time consuming. So we had to force the eye and play a few tricks. Planning everything required together, up front, will result in a better end product that keeps the interest and could be considered a piece of artwork.

There are some great videos showing the Blue Train in action and these helps us choose the right location. In order to we act in est on luxury accommodation grand out tio no le food and k. looked ut o he and sa I sa the ss scenery o g d w out ee g t av. The line from Cape To to Pretc is 00 long and the Blue Train takes thirty-one hours to traverse this distance.

As a result of video and photographic research we homed in on the Western Cape northern borders as you head to the diamond town of Kimberley. Called the Great Karoo, it is a semi-desert plateau of shallow-cut river valleys and untamed wilderness, akin to the Australian outback.

Solving the track gauge problem was achieved by lifting the track onto a long embankment. This pushed the rails into an oblique to the eye and as a result it became harder to determine distances between the rails and allowed us to take the cheaper, quicker way out using UK Peco track. We also convinced ourselves that wooden sleepers are okay here as it's not a termite area, although there are threats to source 1:87 scale insects.

We wanted to experiment with overhead wires on the lines for the first time as a Club. When looking at a layout from above the hard work gets absorbed in the scenic display. Because we were forcing a low frontal view with the embankment, we could silhouette these against the skyline along with the rolling stock. We wanted to use a moving roadway, so the embankment helped there as well, allowing underbridges to be constructed for a hidden return of vehicles on the circuit.

Finally, we needed to cater for the innovative lighting rig on the baseboards. The arid foothills were constructed with forced perspective allowing the colour LED strip to run along a gully, uplighting against the skyline backboard.

The Blue Train running through the Karoo National Park on the line from Cape Town to Pretoria via Kimberley. In this example, the train is diesel propelled, but for the section of line proposed we would be running Lima Class 5E electro locomotives under wires. Long lived and painted in blue livery for the Blue Train, these locomotives were built at the Vulcan Foundry SA in the late 1950s under English Electric licence. (*Shine 2010 Flikr CC by 2.0*)

For the whole display the trackbed is raised, showcasing the lighting effect. This embankment allows a river and working roadway to pass under it as well.

It is as simple as ensuring that the top and bottom ply sections overlap and that the line is offset to the back. Because the viewing is a forced panorama, the public view is an oblique of the front of the embankment only – the rear does not require completion.

Next a substrate of cork sheeting. This serves a dual purpose, to raise the trackbed for a more realistic profile and to provide a degree of sound insulation. There are pre-ballasted track systems or foam underlays with ballast attached which can take out some of the work here if desired. When a baseboard has no insulation layer, be prepared for headaches, they make wonderful sound emitters.

There are several ways of cutting track. The fine-toothed 'Exacto' type manual saw is favoured by some, although it incurs a bit of vigorous work manually on nickel silver rail. Alternatively you can use a circular cutter on a modelling drill. Safety first: eye protection and not breathing in the fine cutting dust become order of the day.

The single-track embankment of the extreme southern (right) board of an eventual total of four baseboards. The track is raised 8cm above the nominal baseboard height and alongside will be fences plus a colour light signal to protect entry to the passing loop further down the layout. The large gap in supports is to allow the shallow sandy river to meander underneath a lattice girder bridge. Single line overhead wires are also to be added.

North Cape, Kimberley : model road

It was decided that with the South African model we would as a Club take the opportunity to venture into the concept of moving model vehicles for the first time. Some members had seen this at exhibition and others had experience of the Minic Motorways system from the 1960s. The latter was regarded as adequate detail for the comparable models of those days, but the slot concept would not satisfy today's…

Alternatives were considered: a physical pulling guide wire, underboard magnets on a pulley system, 3D-printed chain guides. All were rejected as viable options due to too many moving parts, problems with level of detail or quality of operation.

The grandfather of the model moving road concept. The Triang Minic brand had several branches – model ships in 1:400 scale and 1:72 OO motorways perhaps being the best known. The range expanded from the early 1960s to include railway crossings, four-way roundabouts and route switching, and combined other model ranges as the company purchased its competitors. Eventually attention switched to Scalextric racing sets in 1:32 scale as the excitement involved led to far better sales. (*The-saleroom.com*)

It can be perceived as quite a financial outlay for a single moving vehicle, but certain fixed assets are being purchased at the same time. More vehicles = lower cost per car. At least that is how it is explained to the family. The Faller set comes with a recharger (specialist end pins), a single vehicle with a battery, two lots of 5m bare wire for vehicle pathing, a tub of filler for the road wire slot and for making the road surface more undulating, a plastic spatula, high adhesion paint for the road surface (to work with soft rubber tyres), 'Armco' road barriers for corners, road marker poles and road marking transfers. All in all, with this simple setup no other accessory would be needed, so this is deemed as a single outlay.

Above: The underside of the white van. The 'follow the wire' front axle has steering and vertical travel. Use of electromagnets can stop the vehicle or divert it to another road wire if needed. We kept it simple for this first outing. The battery charge is for approximately thirty minutes duration before a recharge is needed (depending on hills and length of track) and full charge takes seven hours. However, a one-hour charge will suffice to get it moving again. We will need more than one.

Right: Test running the van on a 'there and back' loop on a single board. The cardboard road is a temporary affair and allows for different geometry to be tested. The steel line is just taped into place. The van runs purely from a magnet guiding the steering. Being self-propelled, if the vehicle loses the track, it will continue straight over the edge. Therefore, any roadscape will need to have the Armco crash barriers at the corners and a wall or other barrier to prevent a vehicle performing a very hurried vertical exit. Fortunately, a lesson learned before any damage was done.

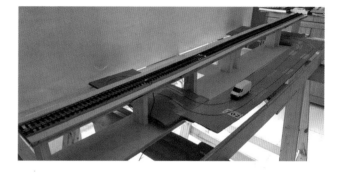

The decision was made to purchase a 'White Van' starter set from Faller and create a simple single board road display.

The Karoo semi-desert location would mean traffic levels would naturally be low, with no complex urban areas to traverse. The single line embankment board was selected as it has a girder bridge over water and the road can occupy a low road bridge in similar profile. This means that road vehicles will be exposed to a silhouetted skyscape along with the girder bridge structure. It also allows for a return loop of the roadway at either end under the railway and behind the backscene.

Overhead wires

Electrification of the railways is increasing and as you move to more modern image British or Continental modelling, you will reach a stage where you may decide to introduce catenary.

Having experimented with 3D printing it was found that the plastics involved lacked strength or snapped if hit accidentally. The systems provided by a number of firms such as Piko (basic) or Sommerfeldt (detailed and compensated) are more robust and if desired can be wired up to become a physical live 12V feed. Electro locomotive models are often switch wired to take live feed either from the track or from the pantograph.

For the South African layout we would be running a combination of electric and diesel prototypes so it was decided that the overheads would be for display only, but touch contact by pantographs was important for the displayed silhouette in sunset conditions.

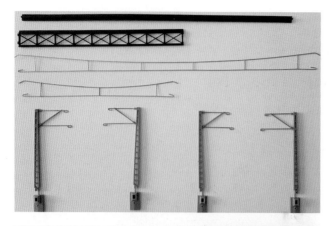

A detailed Piko pantograph, compensated and balanced just like the prototype. The Lima examples for SA electro locomotives will be replaced with a better detailed example like this.

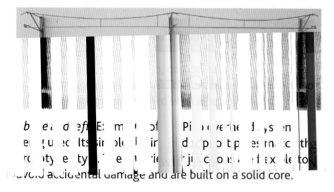

b e: d ef E: m of Pi veh 1 ys n
e ;u c Its ir l ir d p tp es rn c th
r ty e ty e rie j c o l ex le to
vo.d accidental damage and are built on a solid core.

N gauge American: Gila Canyon 1957

Club member Alan Hancock has a long established experience with American outline N gauge. He has two personal layouts that attend exhibitions under the Club banner. British 2mm is different from the American version which is to a more accurate scale. Simple things such as the spacing of sleepers (American spiked sleepers are closer together than British chaired sleepers) are often pointed out when on public display. The Atlas code 55 rail used is also different to the UK equivalent code 55 from Peco.

One of the great things is the ability to keep everything on a pair of lightweight boards suitable for storage or placing in the tailgate of a car with the rear seats down.

The following are suggestions with regards to the generic use of N gauge, not just the American outline of this project.

- Ensure when you lay curves to make them as generous as possible, especially if flexitrack is being used. Most N stock will go around quite sharp curves, but there are exceptions. It can be very frustrating to have a new favourite recently purchased, only to discover that it will not make the radius without sticking or derailment.
- Use the best equipment possible. N scale has improved greatly over recent years, and it can be a false economy to purchase older rolling stock as it may not run smoothly. Motors, compensation of bodies, method of insulation and pickups have all changed. The most modern are expensive but will run well and also have space for reduced-size chips for DCC control if desired.
- Use fine code 55 rail at front of house. It is aesthetically pleasing and looks far more in eeng de c er s ca be c c he s fo ld ar nd nar nd

Tracklaying and scenic build-up is quick, especially when there is a specific limitation on the display framing, in this case by a box canyon. Made from cut polystyrene packing, the cliffs can then be plaster covered and painted. The USA has a huge number of scenarios, from heavy urban industry through to small town desert that can be taken advantage of. Likewise the number of products available internationally via the internet is very large. There is often a quality difference at this scale: American locomotives feel solid and usually have all-wheel electrical pickup which aids smooth and dependable running. (*Alan Hancock*)

The scale lends itself to cameos. Here a trestle viaduct is being built allowing the high freight bypass line to make an appearance. While underboard point motors were mounted on this layout, future builds will have surface mounted motors for ease of installation and maintenance. The older you get the less willing you are to throw yourself around on a hard floor to snag a wiring problem. It pays to think ahead. Flexible track was pinned and PVA glued into place on top of a double layer of cork. The sound-deadening properties are needed even at this scale and rolling stock weight. Cutouts in cork are made for point rodding. (*Alan Hancock*)

It has been discovered that 'electrofrog' points in this scale work far better than the insulated type. The reason is that larger scales have a degree of inertia to get a locomotive over the dead section, but in N the locomotives are not heavy enough to compensate in this way.

Don't be tempted to cram in as much track as possible just because it is possible to do so. One of the advantages of N scale is that scale-length trains can be run in a meaningful landscape. Too much track can destroy this illusion and you end up just looking like a truck storage siding (unless that is your desire).

It is easy to set up a constant running loop and have another as an avoiding line to perform detailed actions to sidings. This can please children by always having something moving. If you want to do shunting, choose a coupling system rather than the chunky plastic knuckle couplers supplied as standard. This will allow you to do some hands-off uncoupling by ramp or magnet.

Be aware, this is not the ideal scale for younger children, due to the difficulty in rerailing and sections that sometimes require deft transformer work. For a parent or grandparent to proudly prepare something that is then promptly broken or ignored as too fiddly can be personally devastating. At the other end of the age spectrum, the more elderly with sight or handling problems should also shy away from building such a layout, since the scale work required at this small size can be very frustrating and prone to accidental damage.

A busy 1950s scene in the Southwestern USA as created by someone who confessed he has only ever stepped into the country once via a bridge from Canada. It is mentioned by North American visitors at exhibitions that the look and feel is just right, capturing the spirit of the times. It proves that if you like something you have not physically seen, working from books and films can be just as good as going there. (*Alan Hancock*)

Rural railroads in the USA are peppered with open level or grade crossings, allowing roads to progress to industrial or settlement areas. This includes sections of the line that operate important trains on roadways at slow speeds such as Amtrack passenger services in Ashland, Virginia or long freight trains in La Grange, Kentucky. (*Alan Hancock*)

Butterwick Extension: O Gauge

Once the Butterwick slot-in board was constructed it had to be offered up to the two existing boards and drilled/bolted into place to ensure that the new track was correctly oriented. The other two boards will remain untouched as they can still be displayed in short two-board format without the engine shed and platform extension.

To bring interest without overwhelming the eye, the new board also requires a two-track bridge deck to be put in place, taking it over a water mill leat. The track going over this will be unballasted and supported on timber baulks laid down on the 3D printed steel bridge bed members.

A new isolated frog turnout was required to feed a siding into the coaling stage, engine shed and inspection pit. Space constraints dictated that a single locomotive would be in residence at any one time, so no isolating section was needed on the siding.

There is no underlay of cork, so like the original boards it will unfortunately be noisy. In common with the original construction, the track will be pinned and glued with PVA, then consolidated by the ballast having a diluted PVA glue mix applied to fix it.

Above left: Adding power drop wires prior to fixing the track into place. This is to allow for power continuity. The wires and holes will be hidden by the ballast.

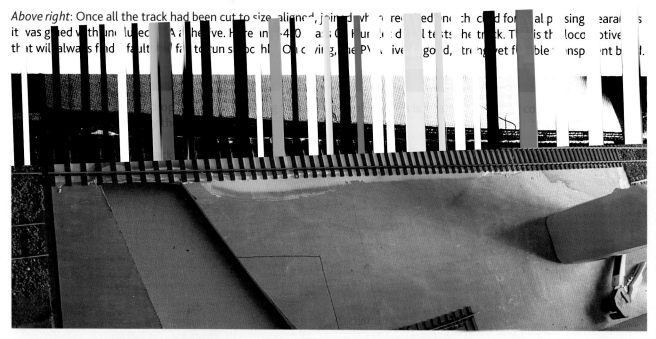

Above right: Once all the track had been cut to size, aligned, joined where required, notch cut for final passing clearances it was glued with undiluted PVA adhesive. Here an S-430 and a Q class would test the track. This is the locomotive that will always find a fault if it failed to run smoothly. Once curing, the PVA gives a good, strong yet flexible transparent bond.

A new platform section was constructed from wood blocks and 5mm ply to copy the original platforms. Resin stone walls were reused from elsewhere on the layout (being replaced by new 3D printed walls) to enable the original components to match the new for the platform edge. A gap has been left where the lighter weight wooden surfaced platform would exist over the top of the stream/bridge and steel uprights will form the platform face. This is linked to memories of commuting days around Waterloo East station, where wood platform examples could be witnessed at a number of locations. This track as the main load bearer for stationary stock at the platform would have a firm packed base on the bridge deck and is to be ballasted. The other track as the runaround loop would be deemed to have a transitory loading by the supervising engineer and thus has a lighter, unballasted build, giving a feeling of depth.

Ballasting in O gauge is a bit easier than in smaller scales. When you use brush or finger, it tends to stay where you want it. Spraying with water with a little washing up liquid added prepares the stone (a mixed colour batch to represent dirtier branch aggregates) and allows capillary action with the glue to make sure it adheres in depth.

The next step is to use diluted PVA – I find a three part water to one part mix works well. Always include a small drop of washing up liquid here as it aids mixing to a smooth consistency. Be aware that if you put too much liquid in, turnouts can become a challenge, both for switch movement and for electrical conductivity since a fine glue layer can be introduced.

'Last chance saloon'. A quick final tidy up with a brush to move any floated stones back into place and add any other topographic features that are desired. For example, where a line of point rodding is to go, an ice lolly stick was used to force a level along the ballast prior to the glue drying.

As this represented a branch line in its later days, some degree of dereliction was required. In the area where any drainage would have been blocked over the years, scrub is shown growing by letting in pre-made nylon tufts to represent early summer grass growth. The ends of the sidings already have overgrowth in place so this harmonises with the existing detailing.

The next addition is the painting with a weathered wood colour. The age of track here would represent much original timberwork – wood greys as the creosote retreats and the desire is to replicate this look.

When weathering or 'adulterating' the trackbed, it is important to ensure several things. Firstly, that you do not swamp it with thick glue after the initial track locating. While you want the ballast to adhere you do not need a thick matrix for it to do so. Be careful near points/turnouts – ballast can obstruct mechanisms and will also prevent electrical contact. Use an 'electrolube' on fishplates before ballasting to keep the glue out.

When weathering sleepers, adding rust and suchlike, you need to be aware of contact faces on points and to keep the upper and inner top faces of the rail clean. This is to ensure clean pickup of current by locomotives. Also, over time, packed on dirt from excess paint can appear on the wheel flanges of rolling stock leading to bad running. Our club maxim, 'moderation in all things' is the order of the day.

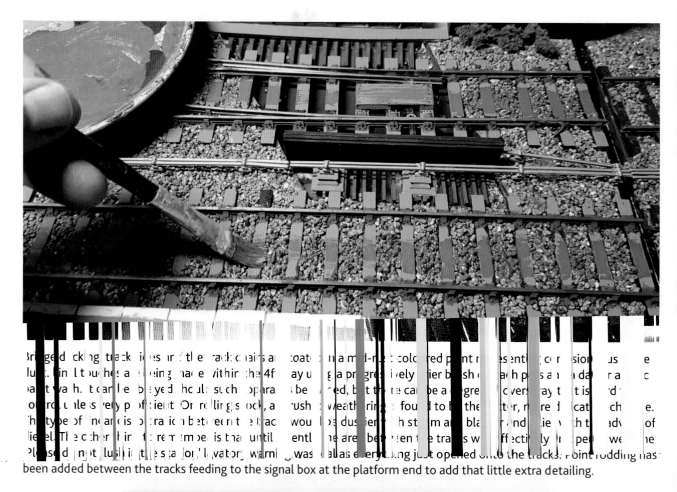

been added between the tracks feeding to the signal box at the platform end to add that little extra detailing.

Finally, the piles of ash and clinker around the small shed and coaling stage are represented by breaking into a domestic water filter cartridge to get the fine material. It can be seen here just prior to the final darkening for the part-burned coal that would be thrown to the side or painting grey through pink for the highly combusted ashpan and smokebox load that would tend to be between the tracks.

An example of a branch with siding tracks slipping into dereliction. Seen here is the entrance to the old locomotive disposal sidings hidden behind Southall MPD shed, water tower and coaling stage. This used to have large water softening towers in front of it and a coaling ramp. The sidings here contained three long, sad rows of GWR steam locomotives in 1963, as mass disposals took place in the Western Region London Division and the diesel hydraulics took over. Later it became a diesel multiple unit depot and the dust and clinker around the tracks was made swampy by diesel fuel as the DMU tanks were always being overfilled. To the left, the Brentford branch runs to the historic Three Bridges site in Hanwell and the site of the old AEC bus factory. A West Waste train of empty domestic waste containers dazzles with its headlight as it runs onto the branch next to the site of the Maypole margarine factory sidings, heading to the waste transfer station behind the A4 Great West Road. Meanwhile, Jubilee 45690 *Leander* comes on shed from the main line with a maroon rake of Mk1s. The September 1997 Southall rail crash occurred on an all lines crossover just the other side of the water tower. (*David Strachan/GWRPG*)

Market Deeping Club motive power depot showcase layout, Obthorpe MPD, prior to full weathering phase. It is always good to see trackwork on a layout without rolling stock present. If it catches the eye and feels right in its most simplistic display form, then adding the moving detail improves the scene rather than hides problems.

Fiddle Yards

The fiddle yard is your stock storage and turnaround facility for your model. Not all layouts will need this – if you have a circular layout or an end to end with scenic locations then it is self-contained and probably you can do without one.

The baseboard construction will be generally similar to your main scenic boards, however you would be covering the board fully with sheet material. Wiring and motors can remain exposed for ease of construction and maintenance. The basic fiddle yard looks rather like a traditional marshalling yard or sidings, such as may be seen on the Club Amberdale and Sutterton layouts.

For larger scales there is the option of feeding into purpose-built cassettes rather than trackwork. These can then be removed or shuffled to provide return trains facing in the correct direction. EM layout Woodcroft has these at both ends since its Edwardian trains are of a limited length. The Butterwick O layout has a long cassette and the Wroxteter O garden layout also makes use of this technique with short cassettes to turn locomotives on a spur at the ends of the sheds. Cassettes save on expensive trackwork, motors and wiring and are also efficient for space as the turnouts themselves are linear space consumers. The downside is that rolling stock is exposed to extra handling, some of which may be off baseboard.

Even if you do have a full fiddle yard, you could mix it with a cassette rail spur to reduce manual handling when introducing/removing stock.

Above left: The Market Deeping Club layout Amberdale control panel, showing the controls round both fiddle yard with real life is a mixture of through and dead end sidings mostly controlled by the operator.

Left: the business end of Amberdale showing a passing train or loco pruning what as a different Seep point motor and wiring all clearly visible. On the main scenic layout, point motors are rather more expensive, slow operation type, closer to prototype operation and under the board.

Below: EM (4mm) scale rolling stock on the Peterborough end of the Woodcroft layout. Cassettes of several lengths are used and normally movement and rotation is performed within the confines of the board to avoid accidental drop damage. There are wooden blocks with bronze tab springs at either end when doing this to prevent stock rolling out.

Above left: Example of an O gauge cassette as used on a garden layout. These are very robust as models can weigh several kilos. They are made from aluminium angle set at the correct gauge width and with spacing washers underneath to ensure that flanges are kept off the wood base. End caps are made from cut-to-size pieces of hard foam packing that squeeze into the gap securely. Leather or fabric handles are added to lift the heavy locos, since they are effectively a straight arm lift at near shoulder height and otherwise in danger of being dropped. Here is a heavy GWR Springside kit of a 43xx 2-6-0 Mogul No. 4356. On the layout itself another short angle piece is attached to the track end and this takes the track power supply. Electrical continuity to these cassettes is as simple as using bulldog clips either side.

Above right: Minerva Models Peckett 0-4-0 tank set up for O gauge Market Obthorpe fiddle concept testing. This style of cassette makes use of a length of flexitrack in a wooden frame. Electrical connectivity is via copper rods through locator tubes either side.

Right: Operator's view from the fiddle yard end of the Club's Market Obthorpe layout. All trackwork is hand built with materials and design representing NER practice. We envisage on a running day that we will need a minimum of six cassettes to keep manhandling to a minimum.

6

Electrics and Wiring

Taken as a whole, the cat's cradle of wiring seen on a completed layout appears daunting and impossible. But with planning, understanding and progressive introduction of complexity you can do it. Seen here under a plethora of wires on 13 August 1978 is English Electric 86 260 (E3114) heading south on the main line at Stoke-on-Trent. The strange notch at the base of the Trent and Mersey bridge beam is to allow the end of a canal lock gate to swing by unobstructed. The graffiti-advertised Joiners Square is now a play park. (*Online Transport Archive Wickens 2987*)

When building up your collection of rolling stock for your layout you have made a decision whether to run traditional DC or to bring in modern computerised controls for locomotive and accessory power, light and sound using DCC. Regardless of that decision, you will have to be exposed to some wiring and soldering to make the layout operational.

This chapter takes you through some of the basics involved. The power operating on modern models is a low voltage and, while it can create small sparks in the dark at times, you will not be getting a painful or dangerous shock from it. However, at the Club we always ensure that our transformers and associated equipment connect to the mains using an RCD (residual current device) plug. While this is not a high wattage electric lawn mower being used, the input is still mains voltage and a potential danger to life if it earths through you or a loved one. An RCD will protect against hardware failure, miswiring or wire breakage which could happen, especially with older equipment. Modern houses have these and a second may not be required.

If you are not investing in a lot of manual connectors and crimped end points you may need to indulge in soldering, which is hot work. The melting point of solder that needs to be reached by the iron will burn you if you touch or drip, plus the chemicals in fluxes are acid, and when liquid are also dangerous to ingest.

It is useful to practise soldering on scraps of metal and different sizes of wire. You soon discover the transmissibility of heat though a short copper wire if accidentally holding the other end! When you get the hang of it, the reward is the deep satisfaction of a job well done.

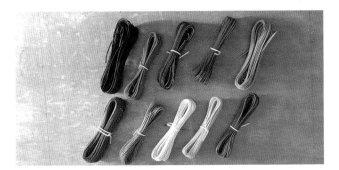

The contents of an electronic wire kit purchased online. Ten different colours allow for recognition of different wiring requirements. There is 5m overall length, which is adequate for a board to be wired up. The core is multi-stranded and the external insulation is soft, allowing for flexibility and easy stripping. The temptation often exists to save money and recycle left-over domestic wiring. However, a project could end up being very frustrating if reusing wires with a much thicker core with lots of copper strands and just three colours available. It can have its place such as in a common return earthing wire, but our Club experience dictates it is best restricted in use.

DC	
Feed	Red
Return	Black
Section Feed	Red
Section Return	Black
DCC	
Feed	Twisted Pair of Red and Black
Point Motors	
Feed	Yellow
Return	Green
Common return	Grey Speaker Cable
Signals	
Feed	White
Return	Blue

Wiring colour rules published within the MDMRC. All Club layouts conform to the standard regardless of gauge or builders. This is so that different club crews attending exhibitions stand a chance of fault-finding the inevitable dead sections, normally experienced with just five minutes to go before the public flood in.

Right: The wiring notes written on the underside of Butterwick by the original builder. This has proven very useful in adding the new board as the wiring continuity needs to be carried over. It also shows you should not commit to permanent marker until you are happy it all corresponds to your plan.

A new control panel is being built for this layout. This will expand the existing simple switching and help sort out some persistent issues with the lack of a capacitor discharge unit (CDU) for the point solenoids to be thrown correctly.

The Art of Wire Soldering

Unless you are investing in a plethora of electrical clips and crimped connections you may well need to solder for the first time. It is often regarded as an arcane art form, but for electrical purposes (as opposed to construction of brass kits) it is quite straightforward.

You may have inherited a 'big' soldering iron or even a Victorian dumb iron that looks more like a torture implement – these are best left alone. A much smaller, fine-headed iron is needed for this type of work.

Solder is an alloy with a low melting point that when cold provides a firm fix between metals. There are some rules that need to be followed.

1. Both surfaces to be soldered need to be free of grease, corrosion and dirt.
2. Wherever possible, if you can roughen up contact surfaces to provide adhesion, ensure you do so.
3. Adequate heat needs to exist so that the 'heat sink' of the metals involved does not suddenly cool the joint.
4. You need a fine-headed soldering iron.
5. You need to provide a flux which will allow the solder alloy to flow smoothly in the joint.

Personal preferences vary with experience, but a good start point is a fine soldering wire of 60 per cent lead and 40 per cent tin without a flux core. Practise on scrap pieces of rail, brass and wire before performing your

  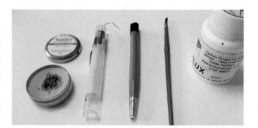

Above left: A method of removing insulation is needed. Shown is a puller type of stripper where the insulation is dragged until in breaks in the grip. There are other techniques including rolling the wire insulation gently under a knife blade to score it if you don't have stripper equipment.

Above centre: Always ensure that you have a method of hanging or docking your hot soldering iron. Yes it has cooled before putting it away. The author is a very recent impress your own compot of hanging how les

Above right: Extras for the job L-R: plain tin is useful to prepare your soldering iron prior to a session before soldering wire, in this case without a flux core; a fibreglass metal cleaning pen; cheap model paint brush liquid flux core aci this case, paste type fluxes are also available).

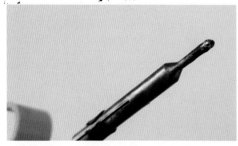  

Above left: When offering the soldering wire up to the iron, do it to an upwards-facing flat face. This allows a pool of liquid solder to form. You can see your iron tip can get a degree of pollution and slag that floats to the side (rather like with full-scale steel founding).

Above centre: Tinning the wire. You do this to bind the core filaments into a single tidy entity after twisting the individual wires together. Add some liquid flux with a brush first – then the solder flows through and ends up smooth and bright. It is best to use multi-core wire as it has more flexibility and adheres better to the rail.

Above right: Using the fibreglass brush pen to abrade the outside of a rail to allow the solder to adhere to a clean, roughened surface. These brushes have a tightly packed group of fibreglass rods to gently prepare the metal. Replacement brushes are available.

final committal to the model. Make sure you are happy with handling the soldering iron and can dock it safely between uses where it will not burn you and it does not damage anything. Determine what you can solder before it reaches the model. Sitting down at a well-lit table is much better than hanging inverted under a baseboard.

The following example shows the steps taken for attaching a simple power continuity drop wire duo on OO track in the Club red and black schema.

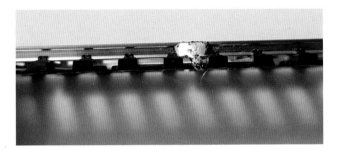

The smaller OO and N rails do not remove too much heat from the soldering site so do not need any pre-heating with the iron. With O and above a pre-heat can assist especially on a cold day. We find it useful to add flux, then flow a base solder into the rail side first.

Add some flux to the metal on the rail and the tinned wire. Add a deposit of solder to the iron, then push the wire gently with the flat of the iron against the base solder layer. You will see the wire bury itself into a smooth joint. Ensure no spoil gets on to the rail top.

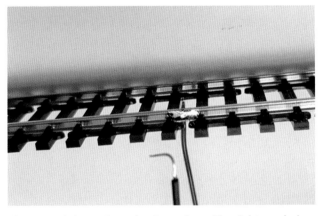

The second drop wire going into place. The right-angled shape allows it to be presented and insulation is well clear of the joint to avoid melting.

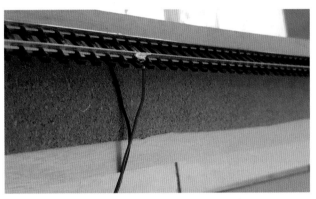

Completed and with a firm connection. The joint is washed with water to remove the flux acid, otherwise nickel silver corrosion could show as a green oxidation contamination in future years.

Low voltage switches for your accessories, fed by a stepped-down accessory feed from a transformer

	Type	Use
	SPST (single pole, single throw)	This is the basic on/off switch – either contact is made or broken. Use it for your layout lighting circuits or operating a specific constant powered accessory.
	SPDT (M) (single pole, double throw, momentary)	Good for use with capacitors and solenoids. The switch is normally centred and you click in one direction or the other to complete the circuit in a passing contact. On release, the switch returns to the centre point again. This means that there is a brief burst of power, ideal for triggering a solenoid on a point motor in a specific direction.

	Type	Use
	SPDT	The centre feed is your inbound live and the switch can either be off by being centred, or activate one of the circuits attached to the outer feeds. You can use this for simple colour light signals (red/green) where you would never have both on. The block colour can vary so you can have red for passing contact, black for on/off, green for colour light signals.
	DPDT (double pole, double throw)	You control two circuits at the same time from a single switch. Using this and wiring four of the six feeds in opposites you could vary the controlling transformer to a line in a non-DCC setup without a conflict occurring, since only one can be live at a time.
	Passing contact, push to make	This is a depression switch which activates a circuit only when the contact is made by positive downward pressure. It can be useful for acting as an isolator on a rail break. Pushing activates transformer power to a siding to release a locomotive, for example. Otherwise it remains off and can protect a line heading to buffers from accidental overruns. The old Hornby Dublo 'Travelling Post Office' used these to selectively power a solenoid on the pickup apparatus.
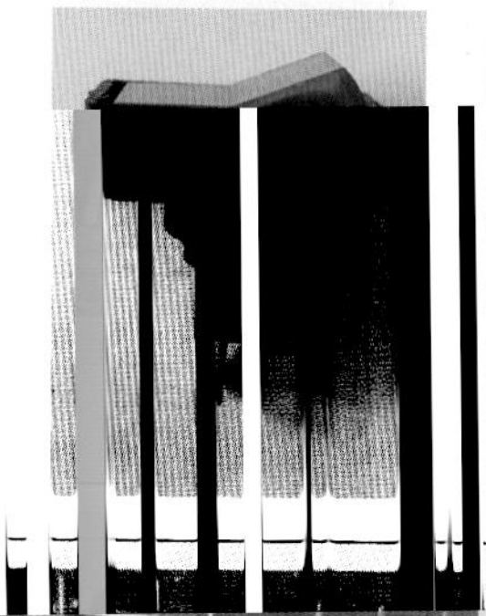	SPST illuminated rocker	You can experiment with using (or repurposing old) automotive 12V switches. For example, a lit switch can be used to show an energised accessory. It has three feeds, one for the accessory circuit and one for the switch light itself, and also an earth for the light.
	SPDT, signal box-style switches	Produced by Hornby to accompany their accessories and in years gone by their precursor Hornby Dublo, as seen here inset on the control panel for the sidings of O gauge Eyton Sidings. These switches are a good option for a signal-box feel. There are more detailed options from companies such as MSE (Model and Signal Engineering) for the more experienced modeller that feel like a challenge (mechanical block instruments anyone?).
	Singe pole multiple select rotary switches	These are to enable a power feed to reach a choice of destination based on the rotary selection. For example, in a complex wiring setup, twelve sidings could be isolated and only one power-controlled by the destination being selected. When you buy these you normally have to also purchase a choice of knob to appear on your control surface.

Power to your Layout

At the dawn of the model railway, JEP (Jouet de Paris) introduced a toy train fed by mains voltage from an overhead wire. It lasted only a few years as it was realised that 230V through a child was not desirable. From then onwards, as manufacturing techniques developed, it was possible to step the voltage down to 12V DC and control the current for speed and direction (reversing the magnetic field on a motor).

There are a lot of good offerings on the market today and some quality older items. However, as with any second-hand purchase it is 'buyer beware' and the older the target the more likely it is that Bakelite (an insulative synthetic resin used extensively in older electrics) and rubber insulation (such as with the older material-

Above: H&M Clipper or Duette (two controls) and remote controls (1970s). They had the option for half wave/current for shunting or slow movements which gave the older style motors a smoother run.

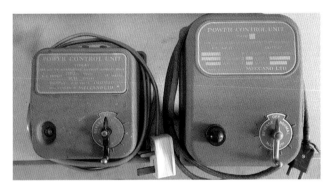

Above: Meccano A2 and A3 controllers from the 1950s/60s for use with tinplate (such as the Club Memory Lane Collection). Robust, smooth, but need safety testing.

Right: More recent Hornby HM2000, introducing LEDs, switched direction and soft touch dials.

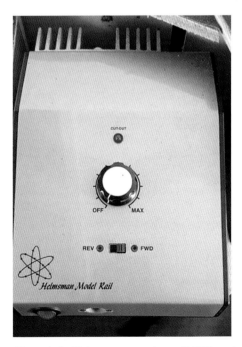

Above left: Helmsman garden rail 5W controller with heat sink. Needed for larger motors with heavier loading.

Above centre: Gaugemaster controller for O gauge at 3W since a diesel model can weigh several kilos.

Above right: On Track controller with a switched slave control enabling remote line operation.

enclosed steam iron type flex) could have perished or been damaged. The danger primarily is mains voltage reaching the outer casing.

What you should be aiming for is a control box that is as recent as the newest technology present in a locomotive on the layout. Thus Meccano is fine for Hornby Dublo and old H&M for Triang and Hornby X04/Ringfield motors. For more recent motor types you will need a more modern and delicate waveform touch to get the best from them without damage. Today you can get analogue (as opposed to DCC digital) transformers with acceleration simulators and other performance tricks.

Points and Signals

On an analogue (non-DCC) layout, to move signals or points you have the choice of either solenoids (which move with a fast snap) or a slower more realistic system of control allowing such extras as slow travel of a semaphore signal accompanied by the bounce of the signal board at the end of its travel.

Back in the 1950s/60s if not using a brass wire to remotely change a point or signal, you were aiming to use an ex-Post Office Telephones solenoid from an exchange being re-equipped. Today you can use the much smaller Peco solenoids with either a passing contact switch or with a capacitor wired in to fire a burst of power to throw the turnout.

If you wish to have slower, more realistic travel there are crawler devices that can be used or chip-based interrupts with preset delays and speeds. You can go as far as having a computerised system that can either load a controller chip or run directly from the screen on a PC or tablet.

Above left: An example of a CDU. Inboard is the accessory power feed from the transformer. Outbound is the feed to the solenoid. The burst when you use a switch or probe gives a dependable result.

Above centre: The trusty Peco PL10 motor. Simple to wire and control. Robust and tolerates variable conditions.

Above right: If you need to, you can combine with a surface mount. Rather than cutting a hole in the board you can distance a board top motor and physically link to the points.

Far left: A 1960s Hornby early two-rail example of a motorised point. Simply, three wires to a controlling switch lever.

Left: Into the 1980s and the Hornby R400 stop home signal. The same lever type and a mechanical circuit breaker to halt the train as a variation.

Right: Up to date. O gauge signal from Dapol. Power feeds and options on switching to operate it from the three extra wires.

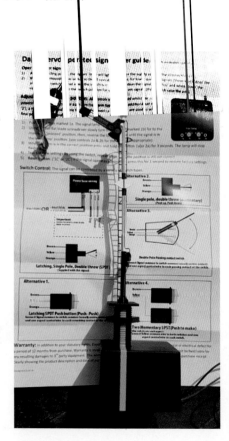

If light signals are being used in place of semaphore, they normally come with explicit instructions regarding how to wire up and control. If more than two aspects are shown on a signal you will be moving towards multi-position rotary switching in order to control them. Today it is even possible to emulate the matrix signalling for platform allocation using LCD displays. It all comes at a cost and a learning curve for the complexity of wiring and control.

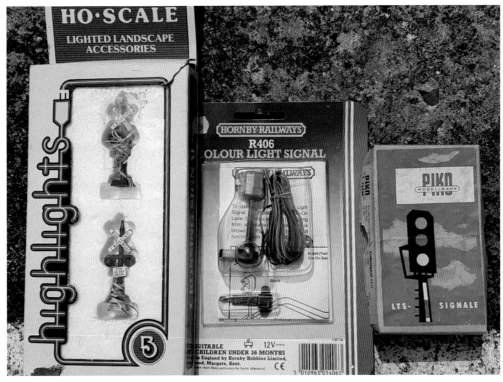

Left: A Peco solenoid-type point motor attached to track and dropped though a slot to the underside of the baseboard. You can see that the earth has been treated as a common return with the top black wires. A SPDT passing contact control switch physically activates one of the two circuits via the CDU, jolting the solenoid to the required position with a momentary burst of power. With these we like to have a separate common return wire to keep the current clean from spikes.

Below: The Peco motor cannot be seen from above. The solenoid throws the switch blades of the turnout with a snapping motion, not a prototypical movement, but the positive movement can assist with maintaining live electrical contact on switch rail.

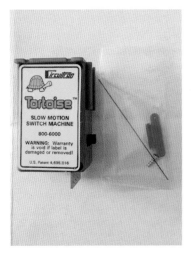

Left: Realistic movement can be gained by the use of a slow motor such as the Tortoise. The throw speed can be adjusted as desired to give a signal-box type physical movement. This also has built in contacts for routing power through to points/switches.

Not everything has to be below the board. For any scale if you are able to mask the position of the point motor then the easier access option is open to you. Here a Peco surface mount is in use. In smaller scales you can have a long control rod or tubed wire from a hiding place deeper in the scenery.

A handy platelayers' hut is acting as the cover. Wiring in this case is below the baseboard, but the physical mechanism is easy to access and there is no danger of water or glue ingress during the ballasting fix stage. A red/white chequer restricted access warning sign is due to be fixed to this building for cast figure health and safety.

Above and left: With cable clips your choice of wiring is fixed neatly into place – any changes require removal and refixing. Us.n 3[rint. to originate e co ect . zed clip and t /s is a useful .nd .ch .m tech i .e. Individua ard lub a e a lo[. .g su. : printi.g f on shared . sg .s i a ne .chno og) w /e. (www. t i.g ve .con

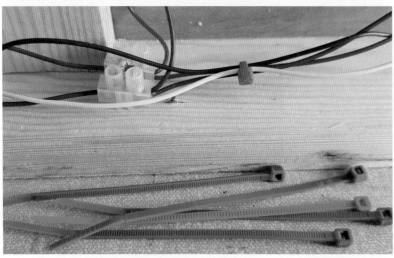

They are called cable ties, although people use them for everything but the purpose they were designed for. In the layout wiring loom, just like in automotive practice, grouping wires, tightening the tie and snipping off the tab results in an organised set of wires. The loom wires can then be twisted together when wiring is finalised to form a tidy loom conduit.

This is Butterwick new board where a simple wiring block interrupt takes the platform line section. The power feed wires (red/black) and common return bus (blue) run to the rail. Brown is through power to the fiddle yard and traverser section and white is power to the loop line section.

Working Out Your Track Circuits

This is the bit in a *How To* book where the author shows how clever he is and everyone else hides in electrical diagram induced fear. Let's break things down into component parts. A busy electrical diagram is made out of many small operations obeying specific rules – it is only when you put it all together that things look complicated. You will be drawing on one requirement at a time and indeed on the layout applying the wires and switches, then testing each, in turn.

Some rules do need to be obeyed. Track voltage and accessory voltage are rarely friends – keep them apart, including any common return earthing. If a power feed came from a specific transformer ideally the return also needs to go that way.

If you get the wires reversed from your transformer to track with your 12V feed all that will happen is that your dial or direction switch on the transformer face will do the opposite of what is desired. Simply swap them over at one end and all will then behave.

As a child the author swapped a 12V DC feed (you can reverse the flow and the locomotive goes the other way) with a 16V AC accessory feed thinking the loco would go faster. Cue the favourite diecast N2 tank loco going up in blue smoke and a lesson learned. In honour of that disastrous event, the examples following are of the rather pretty old Hornby Dublo track, buildings and stock pretending to be state of the art two rail.

An 'entry point' type of basic layout. A single circuit and a single 12V DC transformer power source. The two wires feed the lines. The locomotive has an insulated wheel set feeding the motor and bridging the circuit between the rails.

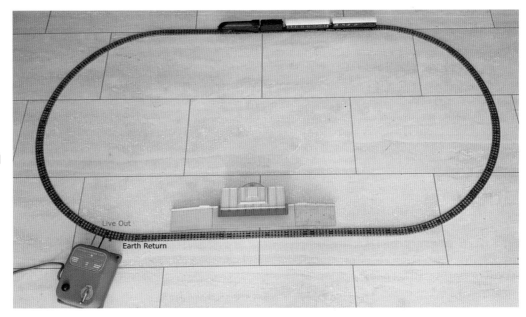

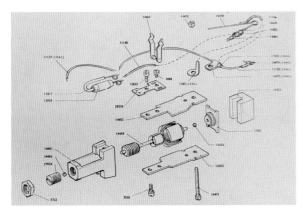 

Above left and above right: How it works in the simplest terms with a 1960 Hornby Dublo two-rail loco. The electrical circuit is fed through pickups on the live side, via a radio interference suppressor, into the carbon brushes which feed the motor armature copper windings. These work to push in a direction within the motor's magnets. The more power the greater the magnetic field. This field rotates clockwise or anticlockwise due to the polarity induced by the DC current direction and speed varies according to the strength of the current. The feed goes back through the wheels on the opposite side onto the return rail and back to the transformer – and off you go, forwards or backwards.

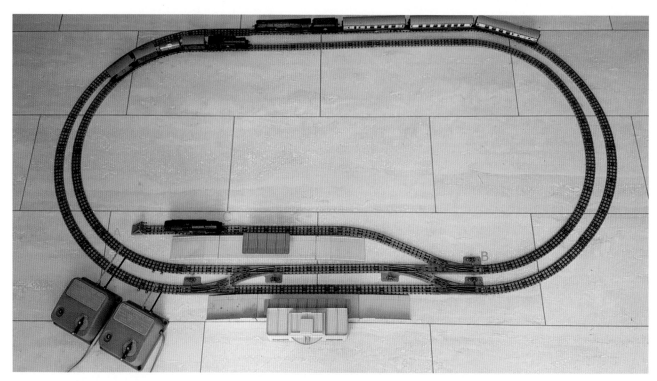

Above: A little more complexity: two transformers and two circuits in action. The layout here has insulated frog points, which means when you throw the turnout switch the opposite line becomes isolated and no current is passed there. Thus at the moment siding C is isolated and the loco will not move. When you use this type of point the transformer wire feed point can be important – you may wish to feed the same line with several wires. The power to siding C when the point is opened will go from A round to B, the long way round, and may bring connectivity issues; if extra wires are fed to B, that would be avoided as a problem. The outer and inner circuit is connected at 1 and 2 – there is no need to isolate as the points do it for you. To move a loco over you'd ensure one transformer is off and the other would guide the train to a stop point to allow reset of the 'road' and normal operation to resume.

Below: The same diagram but this time we have live frog points, which means that whatever direction you switch them they remain live. Power would flow from A to B to feed in both directions when the turnout is opened. This means that the track needs more wiring to control it – isolation between points at 1 and 2, for which you would use nylon fishplates for the lines coming from the frog as its polarity would be incorrect for the unselected direction. You can have microswitch to energise 'at line' when the point moves. At Club, we would also opt for an isolator switch (or push-to-make button) at C to keep that siding inert (dead) when closed.

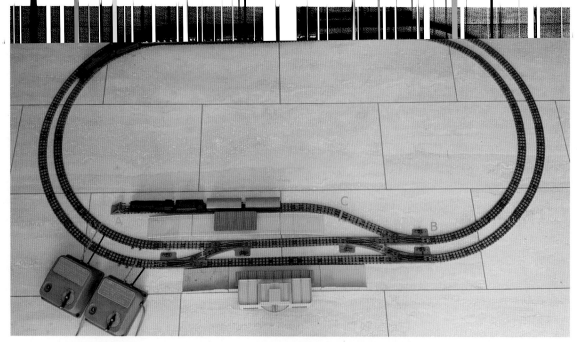

Late 1960s starter sets from Triang had rather crude points and frogs. The author has childhood memories of a friend's layout with the two-axle dockyard shunter – you had to charge around the track to ensure you bridged the gap and didn't get stuck, awaiting a well-aimed prod.

Early Triang example

A large casting in plastic, non conductive area

2 wheel pickup

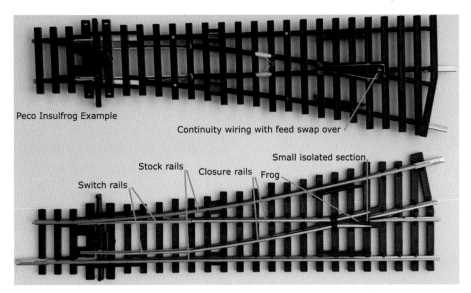

Peco Insulfrog Example

Continuity wiring with feed swap over

Switch rails

Stock rails

Closure rails

Frog

Small isolated section

Why two types of turnout/point? The frog is the 'V' of a point, and the easiest to set up and use is the insulated frog. It has a non-metallic segment separating the feed from the switch rail feed, ensuring the connection with the stock rail is correct for live and return by internal wiring. The reason an electrofrog uninsulated turnout/point would be used is that it has no interruptions of current that would affect slow running or a shorter wheelbase electrical pickup when passing over the point. The downside is that often more control wiring is required, and an insulated connection is needed for both destination rails the other side of the frog as they cannot be both + and - at the same time. The recent introduction of 'Unifrog' points from Peco and other manufacturers alleviates this.

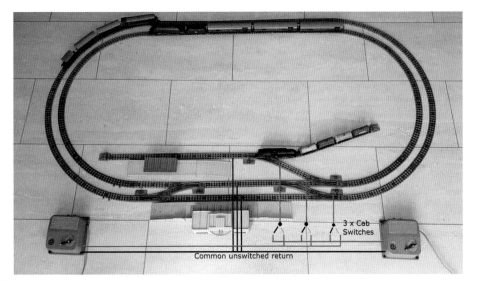

3 x Cab Switches

Common unswitched return

Multi-cab control. Two controllers and three areas. They can each be applied to one of the areas or switched out by the use of a three-way SPDT type switch which allows a feed to A or B, or can be switched out of use. This type of control can be used to give a driver and a roving controller access to a whole line in a controlled manner to control a specific locomotive end to end on a layout. Here we introduce the concept of a common return. This completes the circuit and can be used for AC and DC at varying voltages and should terminate at all power sources to complete their circuits. A feed wire doing a round robin of a layout could be a 'bus' return for track or lighting, points, signals and other accessories, therefore simplifying the overall loom. As a club we choose to keep AC and DC return wires separated.

DCC: Digital Command Control

The Club is divided on DCC – it's fun, it's flexible, it's expensive. The DC crew regard it as a technological moment in time like the old Hornby Zero One or GE ASTRAC systems, and believe that its time will pass and DC, with robust but complex wiring, remains a future constant (plus you can run older locomotives with newer ones). Meantime, the DCC crew enjoy the ability to operate from a hand controller, to shunt locomotives up together or run in tandem, to have sound and lights and a track diagram just for reference.

Having DCC does not mean discontinuing power wiring on a layout, but it does mean simplification of delivery. Ideally you run a single power and return 'bus' round your layout, taking from these spurs to each of your lines and sidings, remembering to be consistent as to positive and negative rails on the layout 'face'.

You can take advantage of electrofrog points with their lack of power interruption but will still need to use nylon isolators on the other side of the frog to maintain consistent polarity. Your power spur from the 'bus' circuit the other side ensures continuation of power delivery.

The execution of DCC is that each locomotive has a unique designation on its chip, therefore 12V power fed constantly to the trackwork is energised within the locomotive itself and a circuit made; likewise directional lights and sound form part of the activation signal. Under the covers this is all binary signalling through the rails at a different frequency, communicating between controller and chip to pull or shut off power on different port settings.

The concept is similar for points and signals. Rather than the locomotive-style chip you have an accessory decoder. This effectively self-learns an address, communicates with the controller for definition and performs the activity that would previously be performed on a control panel. You would run a separate accessory 'bus' wire to keep the power clean.

A common practice is to number the three-digit chip identity on a locomotive as either the class or the cab side running number. This way if your locomotive is a guest on another DCC layout you are able to avoid collision with another locomotive's settings and not have to perform a reset.

If you have an existing DC layout it is possible to convert to DCC but do be prepared to perform some rail cutting to isolate some sections and possibly some track lifting to amend point underside wires to avoid short circuiting. At the same time, you will have to perform full 'bus' rewiring as well. DCC

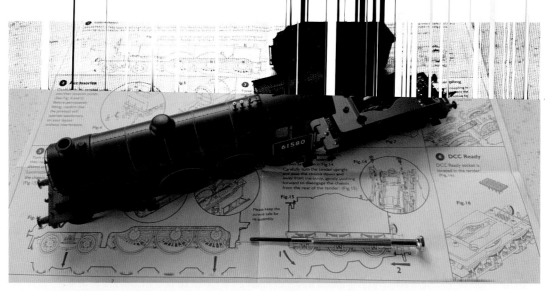

Hornby B12 model being stripped down to show the home of the DCC chip. The tender gives space for a sound cube if desired and the loco can be switched to DCC mode when the chip is loaded. Watch for 'DCC fitted' or 'DCC ready' designations on products, the latter sometimes offered as an after-market service. It's fiddly to deconstruct a modern locomotive so you can opt for someone else to weather the paint finish and set the model up for DCC and sound. To the uninitiated, you need both chip and the intelligent transformer/controller for everything to work. If you push your locomotives hard, be aware that DCC also heats your motors up faster.

controllers do not tolerate short circuits in the same manner as DC transformer controllers, so it can be a frustrating experience.

There are a host of technologies and actuators on the market. If desired, iPhone, iPad or Android devices can be used for cab control, allowing an operator to walk around hands free and follow the train. Admittedly, once you fall into this particular 'rabbit hole' things may never seem the same again.

Lighting the Overall Layout

Decisions on the lighting to be used both over and within a model railway layout are based on the situation of the installation and the overall desire for control of light levels.

If you have taken over a room then it can be enough just to concentrate on the domestic lighting. Perhaps your project can be limited to changing the central room bulb to an LED with daylight wavelengths. The effect of moving away from the yellow hue of a tungsten light source can be quite pronounced – the models you have created, and the rolling stock purchased, will show their true colours. If incorporating lighting within the layout then the ability to also dim this central light source should also be considered. You may also desire to have blackout linings to curtains to run night sequences during daytime.

If your area is within a previously unlit loft space, you can make use of new technologies for your layout and light an area without increasing heat output (especially important in summer even if you have a fully lined loft space).

Garages are often just lit by a bare bulb or fluorescent strip lights. When these are replaced by sealed LED arrays either in bright white or warmer hues, the difference is pronounced. If you take the opportunity to paint the walls white, shadows disappear, which is great for both the construction and operation of a layout.

If lighting a shed, then a lower voltage consumption could be considered. There are 12V step-down options with spotlighters, and battery-driven LEDs which can come with a solar panel recharger. As with all things outdoors, professional mains installation and RCD fusing is a must for your own protection if you are doing a permanent setup.

For portable layouts there are a number of choices. You can just depend on the ambient lighting of where you set up, from window or light sources. You can use transformer-powered LED self-adhesive strips in either white or RGB adjusted full colour. There are, alternatively, sealed robust weatherproof strips which are often used in camping and caravanning.

You can build your own lighting rig to force directional light and shadow using prewired clip lamps. You can make use of a single high

For the North Cape, Kimberley layout, two types of 12V LED strip lighting were procured online. A daylight-wavelength white strip with dimming adjustment and an RGB colour strip with remote control and detailed presets give the ability to create your own colour variations. There are defined cutting points on the strips where the circuit remains intact. On Kimberley, these could be subsequently linked to wires between the four boards to light 5m (16ft) from a single power and control source for each strip.

The white lighting strip was installed inside the top frontage, giving definition control to the moving parts of the layout. At the back the colour strip uplights the scenic backboard and gives the ability to change the mood of the setup. The embankment, when combined with a yet to be added backscene of black hills, will obscure the direct light source to the eye, so that the diffused light graduates, as would a setting sun. We ended up buying commercial connectors to port lighting power between boards – so much easier.

output light source such as a builder's light, which may come with its own freestanding tripod – good for atmospheric shadows.

Above all else, consider your outside lighting as part of your build and the rewards can be marked.

Full front lighting and blue rear uplighting. Bringing in the effect of hard midday overhead desert light, when a sandy/rocky scenic finish is laid, this lighting will accentuate the yellow on the embankment and make the grey of the road hardtop look baked.

Dimmed front lighting and yellow/white rear uplighting, emulating end of day in an arid area. Sky haze or the horizon and lower scattered light flux level.

Front lighting off and rich red uplighting. Sunset hues and enough ambient light to see the rolling stock in partial silhouette. The uplighting rig LEDs will be fronted by a cutout line of black, distant hills backed by tinfoil to increase the colour projection/contrast.

Wiring a Traverser

There are alternative ways in which a traverser could be wired. That chosen will depend on the skills available and the level of operational automation desired.

The most complex method is the use of phosphor bronze contact strips on the underside of the layout. The lines feeding in and out have an energised sprung plunger contact for the live line feed and an earth return common wire used for all lines. As the traverser platform moves, the plunger crosses insulated 'zones' cut across the strip.

The advantage of this is that only the correctly aligned road is energised without intervention. The disadvantage is that it needs more advanced skills to get it working correctly and consistently. Also, the position of the rolling supports for the traverser platform has to be on an inner frame in order to give the space for the wired contacts. Finally, a method of isolating is needed as you do not want sudden live feeds hitting lines as you pass them. This can be done by putting the earth feed through the locator bolts, thus creating a full circuit only when they are located into the correct hole on the other boards.

Because of the small size of this O gauge traverser and the desire for a simple approach, a manual option was chosen. The frame remains a small box and no additional supports were needed for the runners. Switched wiring was used so that the operator physically chooses which line will be active when aligned.

The drop wires from the four lines were colour-coded wires to match the lines and switches. The black earth wire can be seen as a common return passing through each block. The aim is not elegance but robust practicality.

Underside of the control panel showing the common live feed to all switches. We are at 12V here so bare wires are not a problem unless they touch something else and create a short circuit. For finishing and preventing damage, this area was then boxed in by the simple expedient of using part of a plastic food takeaway container cut to shape and screwed into place.

7
Control Panels

Above: Control panels give you the ability to control your layout from a chosen point, reducing the amount of access required and giving a degree of automation. Taken on 12 September 1956 and situated 39 miles 66 chains from the buffer stops at Waterloo the island platform-based signal box of Winchfield had a power panel dating from the 1930s to replace a mechanical frame. This allowed points and signals to be triggered by electrical impulses rather than hard connections to levers. Winchfield is situated between Fleet and Hook on the Southwestern and under the name of Shapley Heath was once the terminus of the line for a year back in 1838. (*Online Transport Archive AND-M327-1*)

Opposite above: The Butterwick layout board-mounted control panel. This demonstrates switching in its simplest form, with controls gathered together for ease of operator access. The switches and diagram need not be high tech but here expansion is difficult so a new control panel will be on the books for this layout. Wires will be intercepted and extended to the off-board box, replacing the current configuration.

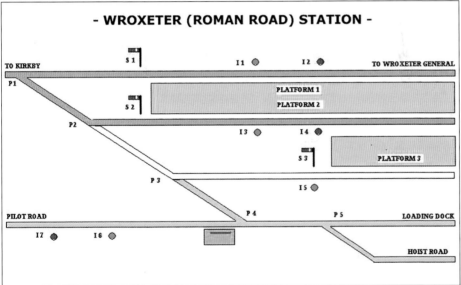

- WROXETER (ROMAN ROAD) STATION -

The signal-box style schema for Wroxeter Roman Road station on the author's garden layout. This was drawn up using a computer graphics package and has the aim of looking similar to the heads-up diagram that most British signal boxes had as standard. It was printed out several times, one for annotation, one for wire planning and one to be plastic thermal encapsulated and used on the control panel face.

The layout wire pairs coming into the parent 'chocolate' block from points, signals and isolating sections. The block is screwed firmly to the baseboard. When running wires along the layout, in this case on boards that were fixed in place first, it is useful to have a defined end anchor point to which to offer the wire ends and maintain a degree of tension without stress on the wire and other jointing. Much of the wiring loom of an old Triumph Vitesse 6 can be seen!

A slightly zoomed-out view. The soldering of wires to the switchwork of the control panel can be performed on the workbench. This is offered up, and wire loomed to meet the child 'chocolate' block. This ensures that the whole facia assembly can be detached for revision or repair without hanging upside down with a hot soldering iron while muttering Anglo Saxon expletives.

The completed control panel facia. The encapsulated print and ply were drilled to accept the bezel nuts of the different switches. It can be seen here that 'push to make circuit' buttons were used for isolating sections, to prevent buffer-end collisions. If unattended, the circuit stays dead unless a button is depressed. The turnout solenoid motors are controlled by passing contact switches and a CDU. Signals are awaiting purchase and installation, thus the blank holes remain.

Market Obthorpe: Complex Control using MERG

Club member Brian Norris is also a member of MERG, the Model Electronics Railway Group, found at https://merg.org.uk/. Their stated aim is to introduce modellers to the use of electronics to control and enhance their layouts. Whether you are using techniques such as DC, DCC or radio control, manual or computer operated, they can help.

Using Brian's experience, we have used a computer-aided system for the Market Obthorpe O gauge layout, defined and working even before the tracklaying took place. This is where a core schema is preloaded onto software, and the result downloaded to be resident on the control panel central 'CANPAN' chip set and the 'CBUS' slave chip units located on each of the boards. These will interpret the associated functions such as moving a point switch or

signal, and also adjust the LED display on the control board facia at the same time.

We started with an AnyRail graphical definition of the layout, which was then mapped to an electric distribution style diagram which logically becomes panel and slave board. This will push slow movement servos, adjust their speed and throw, switch a route and perform track isolation.

Track ends and accidental overruns are protected by isolating sections. We have switchable hub for controllers so an operator can follow a train.

Also how this is a power pack. Everything is well ventilated and mains power is kept as far from the operating way out as possible to ensure full safety. While operators at once show, they are nearly always 30 per cent conversant with a specific layout. Doing this is a standard ensures a degree of protection that is consistent for everybody involved.

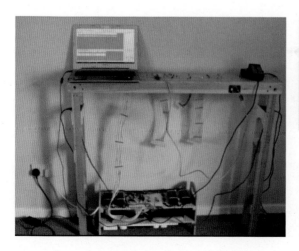

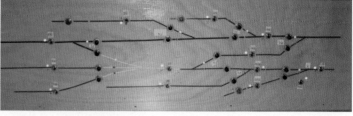

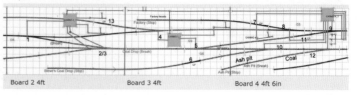

Board 2 4ft   Board 3 4ft   Board 4 4ft 6in

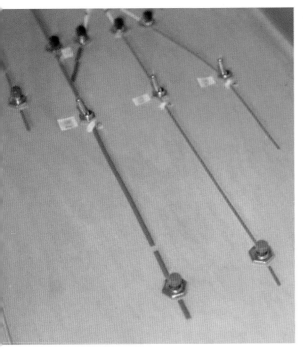

Left: Showing the different colour buttons for point control (black) and the dead sections (red) for the ends of the track which need to be held manually on if you want to run an engine to or away from the end of a track. The yellow LEDs are actually paired with green LEDs so as to indicate which of the two Helmsmann controllers (yellow or green) is controlling the section. The orange LEDs are used for point direction indication.

Right: In operational configuration with the two Helmsman satellite controllers for cab control.

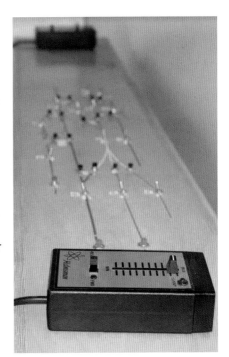

Below: A closer view of the power pack. The overall idea behind this is to keep mains power down on the floor feeding the transformers so that all that comes up to the layout is fed from the transformers and there is no danger of mains voltage being present on the layout itself. (Yes, it could happen and is best avoided!)

Under the bottom shelf is, just visible, a six-way fused connector for the six layout mains power plugs to stay neat when in transit. It is not powered in any way. On the middle shelf can be seen the colouring for the green transformer/ controller. The blue (and yellow) colouring on the top shelf is for the benefit of those assembling the layout to help inform them which 'chocolate' block plugs in where. All feeds from the power block depart from the top shelf.

The yellow umbilical wires are:

- four for traction – two for each of the yellow and green controllers
- four for the CBUS (2 x 12V DC)
- two for the control panel LEDs (12V DC)
- two for building lights etc. (12V DC).

When neat and logically planned, the wiring of a complex layout becomes an asset rather than an obstacle.

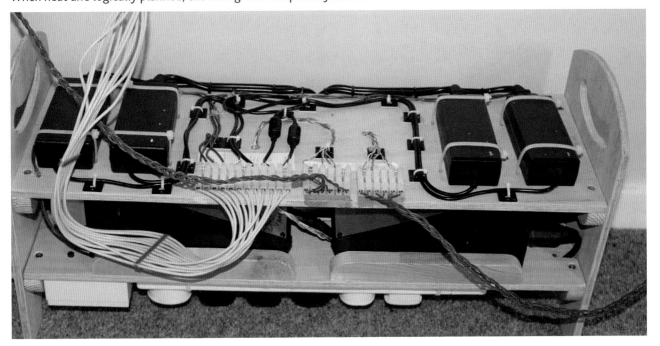

To the left side is the central CANPAN board and legend of the wiring convention. At the base of this are the four connectors out to the individual board CBUS slave boards. Red/blue for 12V DC and black/white for CBUS connections. The eagle eyed may notice a resistor between white (Can Lo) and black (Can Hi): opposite bus ends require a resistor to protect them. The wiring of the CANPAN outputs (in reality, some are inputs) is one of the trickier aspects of the whole job. The wires are split into columns and rows. Some are inputs sensing the switch decisions, some are feeding the panel point direction LEDs. Splitting the pins in this way and then using a multiplexing circuit scheme allows the twenty-four pins on the socket (twenty-five really but ignore one) to be split into two banks of four by eight columns of pins to read thirty-two switches and light up to thirty-two LEDs, which is usually ample for most control panels.

If you enjoy electronics, then this is your Nirvana. If not, then we have included a guide fail to demonstrate what can be done, and you can safely discount it from your plans.

A general shot of an umbilical connection with a wiring list next to it in case of problems. Although all members involved in the project are aware of the technology underlying it, it is important that both a 'desk manual' and annotation on wiring points on control panel and boards exist. It saves rediscovery and frustration when a key person is unavailable. For the home layout, if indulging in a tech solution, as much documentation as possible is desirable. It is amazing how soon you forget key decisions made.

Two more CBUS boards, the 'CANACT' on the left. This is a CBUS 'sniffer' which flashes a blue light if it sees a message on the C (for CAN) and provides reassurance to the user when programming. To the right is the 'CANUSB4'. In both cases, note the connections are four wires, two for DC and two for CBUS. This is common throughout all modules and makes for much simpler wiring, both inter-board and between boards and control panels. Again, there is a terminating resistor on the CANUSB4. This one and the one on the CANPAN would need to be removed if connecting the panel to the layout with terminating resistors added at opposite ends of the layout. Below these is a red circuit board with a blue box. This is the relay which ensures that no power gets through to the servos unless the CBUS boards are already powered. Finally, you can see the red delivery wires to the control board surface switches and LEDs.

This shows one of the CBUS slave unit connections.
- Can Hi
- Can Lo
- +12V
- 0V
- +12V
- 0V

For purists we could have saved a wire here by 'communing' the 0V wires, but we wanted to keep the servo supply as clean (and hence separate) from the board supply as possible.

Although in theory we should have kept these images in the wiring section they go hand in hand with the MERG equipment on the control panel so are included here. A close view of the PCB for a baseboard and its densely packed components/connections. The brown, red and yellow wires are the servo action wires. Rather as with DCC it will only be activated if the requisite control panel hex address is triggered by a switch. So a point will throw, or a signal raise at predetermined speed and bounce, and at the other end an LED will light up showing the activity as well. The PC programming is very straightforward as it is a question of unique assignments being related to the microswitch setting on the PCB representing its hex address.

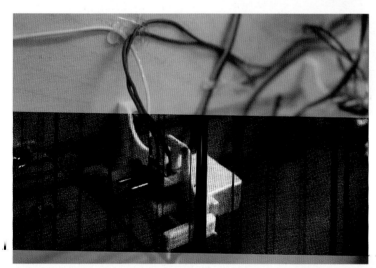

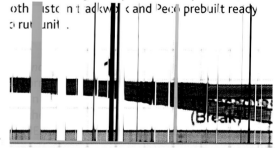

Left and below: A single servo for the station platform line #1 point. The full diagram can be seen in Chapter 3. These servo mechanisms can be either purchased or 3D printed from within the MERG. They have proven to be proficient with oth ustc n t ad kw < and Pec prebuilt ready rut anit .

Right and below: Twin servos covering the three-way point action at 2/3 on the layout diagram These have microswitches to energise the set path, seen as light green, green and orange on the plan. They act in concert when triggered, ensuring a smooth point blade transition.

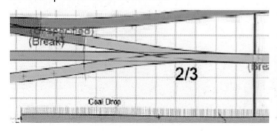

8
The Care and Maintenance Cycle

Above: Trains can travel large scale distances on circuit or garden layouts. Planning a visit to the depot is as important as with the real thing. LMS (ex L&NWR) Oerlikon Watford electrics and LT Bakerloo tube driving car 28217 inside Stonebridge Park depot on 3 May 1947. A towering store of parts and traction motors can be seen to the right-hand side. (*Meredith 9-1 Online Transport Archive*)

Right: Hopefully your facilities for the model railway have a degree of modernity and keep the weather out. Inside gloomy Feltham shed, BRCW Type 3 diesel D6545 (later 33 027 named *Earl Mountbatten of Burma* in 1980) tucked away behind visiting Stanier 8F 2-8-0 48314, allegedly of Willesden shed but missing a shed plate on 26 December 1964. Feltham yard received cross-London freights so multiple region locomotives frequently sojourned there. (*AND-M549-1 Online Transport Archive*)

Congratulations, you have managed to find your way through the minefield that is the model railway hobby. You have a model that is functional and built to the best of your skills at the time of construction. In theory it should all be plain sailing from this point.

As a child I inherited a 1950s Hornby Dublo tabletop layout from older siblings. It was kept in an old Gladstone bag. This would be lifted off the top of the wardrobe in the bedroom by parents willing to sacrifice a quiet Sunday afternoon for one keeping 'tail end Charlie'

happy. Even today the click sound of the diecast crossing gates accompanied by a handful of tinny track takes me straight back.

It would be carefully set out amidst the aroma of old leather and oil and then the first half hour would be spent snagging problems of power and running with a red short circuit lamp on the transformer as a constant companion. Aside from the electrical outages and short circuits, once things were running smoothly, you could run for ten minutes and then a loco would either fall off or stop moving.

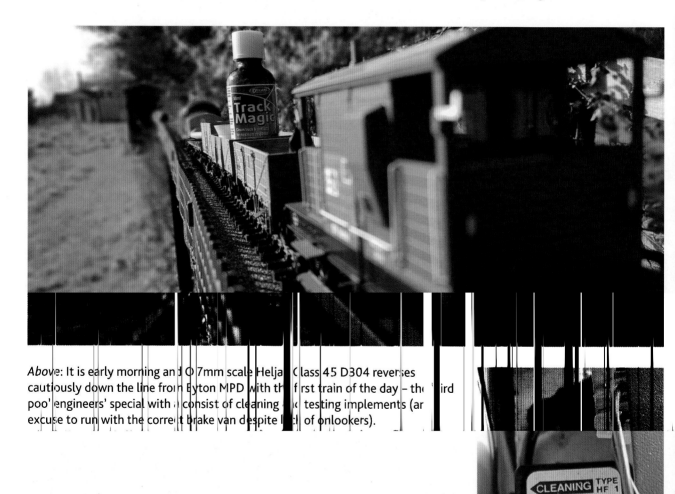

Above: It is early morning and O 7mm scale Heljan Class 45 D304 reverses cautiously down the line from Byton MPD with the first train of the day – the 'ird poo' engineers' special with a consist of cleaning and testing implements (an excuse to run with the correct brake van despite lack of onlookers).

Right: There is a way of cleaning track using a high frequency interrupt device connected from analogue transformer to rail. When an electrical load is applied, the contact point between rail and wheel on a moving locomotive generates a burn-off of dirt and oil. This can be very useful on layouts with inaccessible track areas. The example shown sits behind a transformer on the Wroxeter garden layout which is operating under basic analogue control.

It is not suitable for DCC layouts or DCC chip-fitted locomotives (DCC 'ready' without a chip is OK). The manufacturers state 'any devices connected to the track such as lighting, sound devices or other electronic equipment will cause the unit to shut down'.

I 'regret' to say that the same robust tinplate layout, now seventy years young, is being used by my grandchildren to introduce them to the hobby. They are learning fault finding to get the end rewards of a smooth working circuit. Then, when the apprenticeship is over, they can they hit the expensive stuff as they get older.

Track gets dirty quickly, dry joints appear, rolling stock suddenly squeaks and seizes up and the best looking layout can limp around like a professional footballer after a missed tackle. Constant small levels of maintenance run on a cycle are needed, just like on the real 1:1 scale railway. Even gaps between running can result in problems – it is not just intensive, fast running layouts that can have issues.

Therefore, it would be remiss not to cover maintenance in this book – lubricating, cleaning and such necessities that will enable your layout to run when you want it to and not fail when being shown to others.

Looking After the Track

Mainly you are dealing with electrical connectivity issues caused either by dirt or electrolysis corrosion – the dreaded 'dry joint'.

The primary aids to cleaning track are a rag and isopropyl alcohol, used to lift dirt and oil from the track face (white spirit can be used but does leave a residue). You need to ventilate the area when using either. There are also special cleaning wagons available to scrub the permanent way by running a train over all the track areas, useful for covered sections.

The second line of defence is the trusty track rubber, which is a small, long lasting dense rubber block with metal filings within it. It is mildly abrasive, and the rubber element assists with cleaning. You tend to build up a number of these in your collection since the grey colour blends them in with everything else. Take care on pointwork which can be fragile.

Resist using extreme fluids such as paraffin or petroleum as they will damage your paint and plastics, aside from the combustibility dangers. Do not be tempted to use emery paper or sandpaper, regardless of fineness or grade – it scores the track face and will encourage future build up of dirt.

Many years ago I recovered a Scalextric set from a damp attic to discover a fine rust layer on the track contacts. Having noted that the car pickups run on a fine metal braid I decided that wire wool would be a good cleaning method. It worked very well but left hidden metal chaff everywhere. The first run of a car was splendid until the motor magnets clogged with metal, and everything abruptly stopped. Model locomotives (especially more recent variations) have clip together motor housings that are quick to construct, so this sort of pollution must be avoided. As a result of the construction, pulling apart to maintain and clean can be a dicey business and should only performed in extremis.

Specialist fluids for improving electrical conductivity. These act by dissolving oils and improving metal-to-metal contacts so that wheel-to-rail and rail-to-fishplate remain active. Such fluids are especially useful when track is in place and fully ballasted, preventing frictional movement to re-establish contacts. Fluid can be brushed, swizzled or dripped into place.

A basic circuit testing probe with a crocodile clip. These are a boon on any layout where you have to move away from the transformer to test why something has stopped. Is it the locomotive or the infrastructure that has a problem? Find dry joints and dead sections quickly by clipping to one side of the rails and probing the other to make the full circuit when power is applied.

Sharp-nosed pliers, small screwdrivers and micro files are all useful things to have in your armoury for 'on the spot' repairs. If you do something that creates metallic dust or chaff, ensure you can remove it before it accretes to wheels and motors.

Not just for soldering. The fibreglass brush is great for track revitalisation in difficult areas – it abrades, but gently. It is great for use on wheels to clean up accumulated dirt and dust that builds up on the flanges over time, rather than using a probe or blade.

From the Club Cleaning Cupboard: Things We Currently Use to Keep the Wheels Moving

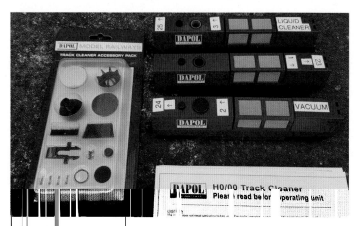

Above left: Several HO/OO Dapol track cleaner solvent and vacuum set. The look a bit like the early AP carriage test jigs used by BREL in the early 1970s. They pick up stray dirt from the track face – very useful in domestic circumstances where fluff and dust prevail.

Above right: Unguents that we use sparingly. Many swear by Goo Gone we use it wisely, from paint spotting to removing oily residues. Trix track cleaner is low residue and good with the N scale RS Components switch cleaner is great for cleaning motor armatures and pickup assemblies.

A Trix locomotive wheel cleaner. It rests underside of the pickups on top of a track section, and you then pass 12V transformer current through the track. The wheels spin on the wire brushes cleaning impacted dirt off the wheel and flange faces, in place of using a pin or screwdriver blade to force caked on dirt off a wheelset while the loco is in a padded sling. The fewer the wheels picking up power the cleaner you need to be.

Appendices

There is always room on your layout for something different. A tunnel-testing train with clerestory coach E940492 at Bourne Station in Lincolnshire, 2 June 1951. Head east from here and there are the Fens, no tunnels to play in. Head west and there is the diminutive Toft tunnel on the Saxby line, completed in 1893. Every tunnel required regular checking and gauging no matter what the length. (*Online Transport Archive Meredith 191-8*)

Association and society websites

16mm Narrow Gauge Association	https://www.16mm.org.uk/
DEMU	Diesel and electric traction – all gauge,. http://www.demu.org.uk/
HRCA	Hornby Railway Collectors Association covering the Meccano years of production, https://hrca.net/
MERG	Model Electronic Railway Group, http://www.merg.org.uk/
NMRA	National Model Railroads Association, covering American railroading, http://www.nmrabr.org.uk/
The 2mm Scale Association	Covering UK N gauge finescale outline, http://www.2mm.org.uk/
The Double O Gauge Association	Caters for 4mm scale 16.5mm gauge UK outline OO and is the largest grouping, http://www.doubleogauge.com/
The EM Gauge Association	18.2 mm finescale, http://www.emgs.org/
The Gauge 1 Model Railway Association	Often described as being a combination of model engineering and railway modelling, http://www.g1mra.com/
The Gauge 3 Society	Supporting and promoting standard gauge railways running on 2.5in track, gauge http://gauge3.org.uk/
The Gauge O Guild	Furthers and promotes standards for 7mm scale O gauge http://www.gauge0guild.com/default.asp
The N Gauge Society	Including British 2.06mm Continental, American 1.9 mm and Japanese 2.03 mm, http://gaugesociety.com/
The Scalefour Society	Covers 4mm finescale with emphasis on track and wheel, https://www.scalefour.org/

Clubs

Clubs you can join and attend or visit their annual shows	http://www.modelrailwayclubs.co.uk/clubs
CMRA	Chiltern Model Railway Association. Maintains a good master list of events, https://www.cmra.org.uk
MDMRC	Our own Market Deeping website. https://www.mdmrc.org/

Useful magazines and other publications

Hornby Magazine	https://www.keymodelworld.com/hornby-magazine
Railway Modeller	https://peco-uk.com/pages/railway-modeller
Continental Modeller	https://peco-uk.com/pages/continental-modeller
BRM British Railway Modelling	https://www.world-of-railways.co.uk/Store/Subscriptions/british-railway-modelling
Garden Rail Magazine	https://www.world-of-railways.co.uk/Store/Subscriptions/garden-rail-magazine
Traction Magazine	https://www.warnersgroup.co.uk/world-of-railways/traction-magazine/
Railways Illustrated	https://www.railwaysillustrated.com/
Back Track	http://pendragonpublishing.co.uk/
Pen & Sword	https://www.pen-and-sword.co.uk/Trains-and-Railways/c/304

Why we 'do' Model Railways

Aspiration is a great emotion. A visit to the Gainsborough MRC by our own Club to see their O gauge King's Cross layout occupying several rooms of an old school building in that town.

Seen here is the eastern portal of King's Cross station as viewed through the front windows. The sheer scale of the layout is incredible. *(Author)*

Market Deeping Club members observing operations in the King's Cross goods depot. The ability to run scale-length trains in complex operation remains a dream for many. To be able to view or participate from a model railway club membership level can take the pressure off the home layout and make it into something more fulfilling. *(Author)*

Market Deeping at exhibition, in this case BR (S) 1960's layout Cannons Cross being filmed by the BBC for the *One Show*, where a broadcast segment represented the recovery of the Club from troubled times. This layout was in store and hurriedly brought back into operation by members to fulfil exhibition duties in place of those layouts destroyed or damaged. Dry joints, warping of boards and points with dead sections all had to be swiftly overcome by a dedicated team. (*MDMRC*)